WHAT WANTS TO BE KNOWN

ADVENTURES AND TEACHINGS OF AN ESOTERIC WARRIOR

by Paul Goodberg
with Linda Sparrowe

Dedicated to
SUSAN PRIOLO
with love
1950–2019

WHAT WANTS TO BE KNOWN
*Adventures and Teachings
of an Esoteric Warrior*

Copyright ©2019 Paul Goodberg
All rights reserved

No part of this book may be reproduced
or transmitted in any form or by any
means, electronic or mechanical, including
photocopying, recording, or by any information
storage and retrieval system, without
permission in writing from the publisher.

Helping Heal the Earth
P.M.B 212, 1001 Bridgeway
Sausalito, CA 94965
www.helpinghealtheearth.org

Developmental Editor: Linda Sparrowe
Cover and Book design:
R&S Art & Publishing, NYC
Photo Credits: Bronx, New York, Andrew
Bologovsky; Cuzco, Peru, Fabio Petti / EyeEm.
Printed by: Blurb Publishing, San Francisco

*Disclaimer: the author and publisher have
made every effort to ensure that the information
in this book is accurate to the best of their
ability and as memory serves.*

CONTENTS

Foreword by Linda Sparrowe 10

Part One The Early Years

Healing Through the Eyes 18
Harry's Generosity 28
When My Family Shattered 32
Teaching on My Own 39

Part Two My Journey to Peru

Healings in the Andes 44
What Took You So Long? 56
Becoming Fearless 67
My Training Comes to an End 77

One last time 84
Lord Pakal and the Nine Lords of Time 97

Part Three Fulfilling My Obligations

Receiving Through Imitation 108
A New Beginning—But of What? 115
Relinquishing My Lineages 117
Dissolving the Occult Triangle 123
Clearing the Killing Fields 135
Liberating the Light Columns 143

Part Four Listening To What
Wants To Be Known

Why What and How I Teach 154
Knowing the Sacred 160
The Practice of Deep Listening 165
The Soul's Journey 170
Our Species Wisdom 173
Wisdom That Has No Name 175

Afterword 177
Acknowledgments 179

FOREWORD

I had heard about Paul Goodberg for years. Friends told me that he preferred to keep to himself, didn't socialize much, and wasn't particularly keen on announcing his gifts to the world at large. Even so, people seemed to gravitate toward him and he was rarely without students to teach and people to heal. They also told me that he was an esoteric warrior, who spent many years living in the spirit world; that he was the head of his family's Central European lineage of Yiddish visionaries and healers, who had settled in the Bronx; that he was a high priest of an ancient pre-Incan tradition and a real cure-the-blind, heal-the-sick, and cast-out-spirits kind of healer. I decided I must meet him.

To say he wasn't anything like I expected would be an understatement. There he stood in the doorway—a short elderly man, a little rumpled, slightly uncomfortable, and so soft spoken I could barely make out what he was saying. Not quite my image of an esoteric warrior/high priest; in fact, he was definitely more Bronx than pre-Incan. And then he opened his mouth. Several hours and many stories later, I began to understand his power. But it was when he invited me into a healing circle with close friends, which continues today, that I began to receive and feel his power. What I have experienced, from that moment on, has been an elder at the height of his esoteric power, who has chosen to remain hidden from view, much like his teachers had before him.

He rarely speaks during a healing, although occasionally he might add a sentence or two before we begin—he finds Westerners need that—but otherwise, all transmissions are telepathic. The healings he offers us may be silently transmitted but they're never ambiguous; they may be intensely potent, but they're always exactly what's needed. That's the traditional way; everything he was given, everything he learned from every one of his teachers, including his Yiddish grandmother, Gussie, the Q'eros high priest don Manuel, and Lord Pakal, a seventh-century Mayan king, was delivered and received telepathically. As a result, he had to learn at a very early age to truly "listen" to what he was being taught, to what wanted to be known. This is key to his teachings, to his ability to heal others and to heal the planet. He listens to what needs to be known, imitating each of his teachers until he is transformed into them, embodying the powers and capacities they have given him, and then uses what he deems appropriate for what has revealed itself.

His students began asking him to put words to the wordless, so that these teachings may be of benefit to others. Now in his mid-seventies, and with no immediate heir, he's finally agreed. His intention is twofold. First, he wishes to chronicle his own relationship with, and participation in, the spirit world and the realm of the Sacred, one which is alternately hazardous and ordinary; life-threatening and life-affirming. Secondly, he wishes to offer practices, gleaned from the wisdom he's been gifted—not just from his teachers, but also from mountains and animals, icons, relics, and sacred places—which will allow us to experience the Sacred in our own lives. Practices that move us "beyond self" to establish and maintain a reciprocal relationship with nature, with "All That Is," which he believes is the first step in recovering our essential humanity.

At first blush, this probably sounds like every other spiritual teacher you've ever heard of, read about, or sat with. I know it did for me. But it isn't. Most spiritual practices move us increasingly inward, toward a deeper relationship with the Sacred, which we may identify as the Self, or Universal Consciousness, or our personal God within. Paul says the Sacred is actually outside of us, not within. He, of course, agrees that it's important to go within, quiet the mind and find stillness—that's how we learn to listen. But if we only focus on the internal aspect of the Sacred, it's too easy to equate the Sacred with self-help. What can meditation do for me? Will reading spiritual texts, practicing gratitude, chanting or walking in nature make me a better, kinder, gentler, more focused person? Me, me, and more me.

In Paul's perspective, which is a traditional one, the natural world represents the most immediate and accessible manifestation of the Sacred, which asks to be met on its own terms; it is "what wants to be known." We can't possibly know what nature needs, he says, until we can experience what nature truly is. No relationship can be sustainable without reciprocity; no meaningful relationship can exist without reverence. Herein lies the problem. In the West, the relationship is based on a "let us fix it" model, which is one sided and has caused great suffering. We project onto nature what we believe she is (and, by extension, what we believe she needs) without waiting for her to show us. Paul's understanding of nature's reality is a mystical one; it's the essence of direct experience, not an inventory of characteristics. The key, he says, is to allow what wants to be known to come to you over time. Be patient. Be still. And listen.

But how do we do that when we have almost no direct experience of the natural world, almost no direct experience with the Sacred? Paul answers that question by reminding us that our ancestors once lived as part of the natural world and believed themselves to be an intimate part of it. That means, he says, that our species is capable of this connection because it is our natural inheritance as humans.

Entering into a reciprocal relationship with the Sacred requires us to reestablish the skill set that is part of this inheritance. That means we must approach the Sacred more as a poet and less as a scientist. We must move toward it, as Paul does, with stillness, a sense of reverence, and without projections. Listen, he says, and the Sacred will reveal itself within the stillness. Not necessarily right away. It may take days, years, decades. But you must look and listen without expectation. The natural world is not human and yet it speaks to our species wisdom. It connects us to the world we are born into and the sacredness of everything around us. But we must stay open and empty and ready to receive.

Paul received these teachings in the most unorthodox way. Honestly, I haven't heard stories and escapades like these since I read Carlos Castaneda's *The Teachings of Don Juan*. But there's nothing fictional about Paul's experiences. Part of what makes his teachings so powerful is the means through which he received them. I encourage you to start from the beginning, from when Paul was first born and his dear grandmother Gussie appeared to him in his hospital bed, without ever walking through the door. Indeed, that's only the beginning! There are so many more escapades, including near death experiences, that Paul relates in the most matter-of-fact, self-effacing manner.

We are grateful for all that he experienced, for all the teachings he has absorbed over his lifetime. And we are fortunate that he's willing to share what he has received, in order for us to enter into a more reciprocal relationship with All That Is, open up to the deeper wisdom we already possess, and begin to understand how we can help heal the planet.

Linda Sparrowe, New York 2019

PART ONE
THE EARLY YEARS

Healing Through The Eyes

My maternal grandmother Gussie Feldman, nee Buden, and her husband Harry, were both Orthodox Jews whose families emigrated from Eastern and Central Europe when they were children—primarily from Poland and Russia—and settled on the Lower East Side in New York, at the turn of the 20th century. By the time I was born Gussie and Harry had been in the Bronx for more than twenty years and had already raised nine children. Gussie came from an ancient lineage of traditional esoteric healers, mostly women, whose silent transmissions healed countless men and women, in the old country and in America. Gussie chose me as her heir—after it became apparent that her daughter Harriet's health would not allow her to assume the mantle herself—and then set out to train me. She was my first teacher.

WHAT WANTS TO BE KNOWN

I honestly don't remember the name of the hospital in the Bronx where I was born, but I do know that Gussie came to visit me there, the day I was born. I was told she arrived, clad entirely in black, of course. Gussie always wore black and she was always covered up, head-to-toe. Whenever she'd leave the house, she'd put on a long black dress and thick black stockings, and hide her hair in a black scarf. That's how she had shown up at the hospital. She showed up because she wanted to give me her blessing, which really was a two-fold gift. First, she freed me from an inheritance of family trauma, the trauma that had come with us from Europe when her family, her husband Harry's family, and my father's family (on both sides) emigrated to the United States. Secondly, she acknowledged me as the heir apparent to the family lineage. With her blessing, I would become the next lineage holder.

One of my earliest memories of Gussie involved a visit she made to my parents' apartment when I was sick with some sort of childhood illness. I must have been about three years old. It was early in the evening and I was lying in my bed when Gussie appeared. It was as though she had walked through the wall. And there she was, suddenly, standing at the foot of my bed, talking to me in Yiddish. My door hadn't opened, she hadn't been ushered into the room by my mother (her daughter). She was saying something like "Don't be frightened. I'm here to give you a heal-

PART ONE: THE EARLY YEARS

ing." But I was frightened! She had just materialized, seemingly out of nowhere. She did give me a healing, I remember that, and I remember feeling better almost instantly. And then she disappeared the same way she had entered—back through the wall. No one seemed the least bit surprised at Gussie's capabilities; my mother and her five sisters were all similarly talented—apparently there was some kind of esoteric inheritance among the women in the family—but not one of them was the least bit interested in being Gussie's heir.

I spent a lot of time as a young child at Gussie and Harry's apartment. I have memories of Gussie picking me up and putting me in a chair at her kitchen table, while she offered a healing. The scenario was the same every time. A person would come to the back door of her kitchen, knock, and then walk in. They'd greet each other with a nod and a "come in, sit down" kind of thing in Yiddish. It was always someone who either knew Gussie or had heard of her because they had to know which alley to go into, which staircase to walk up, and which door to walk through. I don't ever remember seeing a woman or a young person coming into the kitchen for a healing—it was always a man. He would be on her right; I would be on her left; and Gussie would be looking straight ahead. The healing would commence. Gussie never looked at the visitor and never asked any questions; and the visitor never offered any explanation or personal information. In fact, no one ever spoke and nothing ever seemed to happen. And yet the atmosphere in the room was calming, bright and reassuring to my three-year-old self.

All this would go on for, I don't know, maybe five to ten minutes? I don't really know exactly, because there were no clocks in the house and no one ever wore watches. But that's what it felt like. At some point, the man would get up and put a penny or two in the charity box on the table, leave through the back door, down the stairs, into the alley, and back onto the street. The money in the charity box was always donated somewhere to benefit the community—although I have no idea where.

Occasionally, at the end of a healing, Gussie would reach for a glass, fill it with water, and set it down in front of her. It was always the same glass: tall with red, white, and black stripes, which she had bought at Woolworth's or some other five-and-dime in the neighborhood. She'd drop in some salt or tea leaves, stare into it for a moment, and then say something to the man sitting there—usually about his health, his family, or maybe his future. This divination was rarely in response to a question or concern; she would just decide it needed to be done. It was the only time she spoke.

She did anywhere from four to eight healings a week—starting on Sunday and ending on Friday. No one came on Friday night or on Saturday; no one ever came in the evening or before breakfast either. Often, when someone showed up, it was obvious they hadn't eaten anything, so Gussie or Harry would feed them. To say they were poor would be an understatement. They were destitute, a family barely able to make ends meet, one that included nine children. But none of that mattered. They would still feed anyone who came to the door hungry—and in those days there were plenty of hungry people, people for whom the Depression of the 1930s was still a stark reality. We were living in the midst of hundreds of thousands of poor people, really poor in ways that are hard to imagine.

Gussie was a very potent, fluent, and to-the-point spirit healer. She could tell, almost immediately, if someone was in poor physical health, although she never offered healings for specific physical maladies. Her focus was on the vibrational or energetic body; she could read it fluently and had the capability to heal any negativity within it. Obviously, healing what was happening energetically affected the physical body as well, so in that respect Gussie could restore physical health. Just not directly. Gussie's specialty was banishing the evil eye, the curse someone received, often without realizing it, which could harm them energetically or attack them physically. She could remove the negativity, cast out the evil eye, help the person feel better, and keep them free from harm. Her healings could soothe the soul of anyone who was agitated.

WHAT WANTS TO BE KNOWN

Gussie never uttered a word when she offered a healing. She never invoked spirits or deities, although she lived in the spirit world herself. She healed through her eyes, offering energetic gifts directly to the person who needed healing, without ever directly looking at him. The energy would come out of her eyes and fill the whole room; the person would be sitting in it, enveloped in this healing energy; and it did whatever it was supposed to do. And, when the healing was over, the person would stand up and put a little something in the charity box and leave, without saying a word. There really was nothing to say.

I sat in the chair, in that tiny kitchen, countless times, witnessing Gussie's healings. Before I entered kindergarten, I was at their place more than I was at my parents' so Gussie was really a second mother to me and Harry, a second father. After I started school, I spent every weekend with Gussie, and almost every day in the summer. If no healings were taking place, I'd sit on my stool and watch while she cooked or washed the clothes. There was no washing machine, of course, nor was there a refrigerator. Only an icebox, which meant Gussie went to the market every day and I went with her. She'd take me by the hand and we would walk down the street, stopping in at the grocer, the butcher, and whoever else had what she needed to buy that day. She always held my hand. She always talked to me telepathically, whenever we were together, and rarely uttered a word.

PART ONE: THE EARLY YEARS

During the 40s and 50s, the Bronx was a mean and violent place to live. Gussie taught me how to protect myself from attack. How to see people—people who were negative, people who were evil, people whose energy was dark. She taught me how to see illness and health in others, and to remove the evil eye. I became very adept at telepathic communication. I had to, really, because she almost never spoke to me; in turn, I never asked questions or commented. I stayed silent. In Gussie's presence, I felt calm, at ease and relaxed. I was happy and safe.

Gussie also taught me to defend myself in the spirit realm—against attacking spirits and against women and men who commanded spirits to attack me. She was my mentor and protector in the spirit world and, even after her death, she continued to protect me in that realm. I learned how to heal using the powers of the spirit realm. Later, I amused myself in the spirit world by attacking other spirits. All the while, I attended public school, played sports with my buddies, and enjoyed going to the movies.

Gussie and Harry's daughter Harriet still lived at home during the time I was with them. Harriet had been Gussie's designated heir, but as best I could tell, she had had some kind of nervous collapse as a young teenager. She used to look after me sometimes when I was at their apartment. If I wasn't with Gussie, I was with Harriet. Harriet would sit with me in the bathroom because I wasn't allowed to go there alone. The rats in the bathroom were much too big for me and everyone was afraid I'd get bitten. Harriet also made sure I got fed and put to bed. She used to tell me stories, the stories she had been told when she was a child.

In public school, I remember liking my kindergarten teacher, but my first- and second-grade teachers were difficult for me—and I was difficult for them. In second grade, I was already capable of offering healings but not so capable of using my gifts wisely. In fact, I reveled in offering my teacher "reverse" healings. I would come into class in the morning and do the opposite of a healing—causing her to develop terrible headaches. So terrible, in fact, that she finally had to take a leave of absence. A substitute took her place, but her headaches became so debilitating that she left, too. By the time the third substitute took over, I didn't need to do anything because she was only a caretaker and didn't really bother any of us. I kept up these reverse healings all through grade school, with teachers developing all kinds of strange illnesses, and I didn't stop until high school. I finally realized what I was doing was wrong. Initially, though, I justified my actions as a way of protecting myself because I had had a terrible time in school. In time, I realized that what I was doing went against everything Gussie had taught me; I never again misused my gifts to intentionally harm anyone.

PART ONE: THE EARLY YEARS

Over time I became increasingly skilled at offering healings. Never at Gussie's kitchen table, of course. I was always her student. But I would be somewhere where it was obvious to me that someone needed a healing so I would quietly offer it. The more I offered, the better I got.

When I was eight years old or so, I started riding the subway by myself from the Bronx into Manhattan, to go to the movies and music concerts and see exhibits at various museums. I could get free tickets to the New York Philharmonic and the Met opera from my school, and I went as often as possible. By the time I reached fourteen, I was hitting the jazz clubs in Manhattan. I always felt perfectly safe. As I mentioned, Gussie had taught me how to protect myself from any negative energy I encountered, and my dad had taught me how to keep myself safe from harm on the subways. So I had a wonderful time enjoying New York.

There were plenty of people who regularly went to healers like my grandmother. They were woven into the fabric of our community. We had no body workers or acupuncturists, or naturopaths, or any of that sort of thing. Ours was a world of healers and healing and nonverbal communication—the world of central and eastern Europe. And in this world of healers and mystics were Jews, Gypsies, Sufis, and quite possibly Orthodox Christians, although I'm not sure about the Christians. What I do know is that the healings my grandmother offered were similar to what the Roma offered. These were healers who lived in the spirit world and practiced their religion of birth. They all knew each other because they shared a common esoteric practice, and had lived in the same villages before coming to America.

Walking down the street, we would run into people all the time who lived in the spirit world. Just walking down the street. It was that kind of neighborhood. When Gussie and I would go to synagogue, we would sit in the women's section and other women who lived in the spirit realm would be sitting there, too. We all knew one another. When Gussie died, hundreds of people showed up at her funeral—those in the spirit realm as well as others who had been the beneficiaries of her healings. They spoke Yiddish, they spoke Polish, they spoke Russian. They weren't American. They just happened to live in the States.

Harry's Generosity

Within the Bronx was a complex and rich subculture, with a lot of interesting, generous people. In fact, the generosity in the midst of the violence and extreme poverty was quite extraordinary. There were always stores and restaurants where you could show up, when you were down on your luck, and get something to eat or drink. While Gussie taught me the way of the warrior—how to protect myself as I navigated both the neighborhood streets and the spirit world —Gussie's husband, Harry, epitomized that culture of benevolence. He taught me, from a very young age, the importance of generosity.

My mother's family was large and impoverished and Harry supported them all by selling fruits and vegetables from a horse-drawn wagon he'd rent for the day. Each morning, six days a week, he would go to the wholesale market in the Bronx, buy fruits and vegetables, load them on the back of the wagon and peddle his wares through the neighborhood. Somehow he managed to make enough money every day to put food on the table. He couldn't afford the freshest fruits and vegetables, so he'd buy stuff just this side of rotten; it was cheaper and he could sell it at reasonable prices.

When Harry got older, in his mid-50s, it became too difficult for him to steer the wagon and take care of the horse every day. He decided he needed a store. He'd walk the streets of the neighborhood and peer into abandoned storefronts until he found one he liked. Then he and my dad would pick the lock, break into the store, and look around to see if it had electricity and a working refrigerator. If it didn't, they'd lock the door back up and keep looking. If it did, they'd set up shop. He'd stay there, selling his fruits and vegetables until the landlord happened by and demanded to know who the hell he was, what he was doing there, and why he wasn't paying rent. At that point, Harry would move on and find another place.

My dad would often drop me off for the day and I'd hang out with Harry. People would walk by, some of whom I knew by sight, rub my head, tickle me a little, and talk to me in Yiddish—"Look how cute he is!" I'd sit on a stool or stand around, eat some of the fruit, and chat with Harry and his customers, many of whom had no money at all. Harry knew every one of them—and their circumstances. So he'd say, "Here's a little something for you," or "Why don't you take this?" or "Is there anything you need?" He probably gave away as much as he sold. When my dad would come by in the afternoon to pick me up, he'd say to Harry, "Did you sell anything today or did you give it all away?" And, of course, when he heard the answer, he'd say, "How the hell are you going to feed your family if all you do is give stuff away?" My dad was horrified at Harry's behavior because it was important to him that everybody in the family be taken care of first. Nonetheless, if Harry hadn't sold anything that day, my dad would slip him a five or a ten and we'd head toward the subway and make our way home. We were quite poor ourselves, so for my dad to slip him that kind of money was a big deal. Anyway, I hung out with Harry for years, as he supposedly sold fruits and vegetables. His many acts of generosity have informed my own way of being in the world and serving others.

Harry was fond of telling this one story—and he told it often. Although the details would change, the basic story went something like this. After a day's work, Harry returns the horse and wagon as usual—or locks up the store (depending on which version he's sharing). He heads to the subway with the money he's made that day, planning to jump on the train and head home for dinner. After a few blocks, he comes upon a family begging on the street; they're hungry and they have no money. So, he reaches into his pocket, takes out what he has, and gives it all to them. He continues on his way. When he gets to the subway steps, he realizes he has no money left. As he stands there wondering what to do, how he's going to get on the subway, how he's going to get home, what he's going to tell my grandmother, the wind suddenly kicks up and a five-dollar bill flutters in the breeze—right in front of his face. (Sometimes, if he's really trying to make a point, it's a ten-dollar bill.) He snatches it out of the air, walks up the stairs and presents it to the attendant at the cashier's booth, who gives him change and a subway token. He gets home in time for dinner. The point of his story, of course, is that you absolutely have to be generous, no matter what, and your generosity will always be repaid. No matter how painful or impossible it feels, you are responsible for the welfare of others. He must have told me that story fifty times. He wanted me to know that was what our family did, that we believed we were responsible for other people. That it wasn't just about family...it was about everyone.

When My Family Shattered

I was thirteen when Gussie died. She was only 60 and her death destroyed the whole family. We lost our matriarch and no one had the strength to hold this huge family together anymore. The whole family just collapsed. Harry was shattered and so was Harriet. I lost track of both of them for many years. In fact, I didn't see either of them again until I was in my mid-twenties.

When Gussie died, I worried that my training was far from finished. In reality, it was complete, but what was missing was her mentorship and any sort of community context. My access to the esoteric community had been through Gussie. And when she died I lost all that and I was too young to forge any connections on my own. I remember seeing hundreds of people at her funeral, most of whom I recognized by sight. I didn't know their names and I didn't know where they lived or where they worked. And, even if I had known, I certainly didn't feel like I could drop by for a visit. I was just a kid. So I was trained but without a context.

By the time I was in my mid-twenties, Harry had become too old to continue to sell fruits and vegetables and Gussie's youngest son Morty (who called himself Marty outside of the family) took up the mantle of supporting the family. Marty had learned to cook in the Army and he opened a little restaurant that served breakfast and lunch; it had about ten tables and a counter with a few stools. He called it Marty's Luncheonette and Truckstop. I'd go over there often and help out, bussing tables or waiting on customers. Marty cooked and Harriet worked the cash register and took care of the counter.

At the end of the day there was never much in the cash register. I have no idea how many people actually paid for their meals and how many ate for free. Of course, the family was still terribly impoverished and, in reality, Marty's Luncheonette was more of a soup kitchen than restaurant, with just enough breakfasts and lunches sold to truckers and factory workers in the industrial part of the Bronx to pay the rent—most months anyway. Other times, my dad paid it. Marty's Luncheonette went on that way for years until Marty died of a brain aneurysm and there was no one left to cook.

All my life I was taught that generosity was a

moral and ethical imperative—no matter what. I was raised in the context of Gussie feeding people from the neighborhood who were hungry; Harry giving away fruits and vegetables; and Marty preparing food at his restaurant to feed those too poor to pay.

I was glad to see Harriet again. We had a wonderful telepathic communication and there was a lot of affection between us. We'd see each other at the restaurant about once a week and occasionally she'd invite me for Sunday dinner at her apartment and my parents would join us. Harriet never married. She lived alone and she wasn't in great health. She had something wrong with her kidneys, caused by a toxic reaction to a medication she'd been prescribed, so she wasn't well.

One evening, Harriet hosted my parents, Dotty and Jack, and my wife at the time, Lucille Taylor, and I for dinner. I think I was about 30 at the time. After Harriet had served dinner without dessert—she never served dessert, which I always thought was odd—she announced that there was something special and unusual she wanted to do. I wasn't really paying much attention. It was one of those dinners where I had eaten too much and was feeling kind of lethargic. Also, the atmosphere was a bit tense. No one in my family really liked Lucille (she was my second wife); she wasn't Jewish. She felt ill at ease with them, too, and of course, I was picking up on all that energy, so I was also pretty uncomfortable.

WHAT WANTS TO BE KNOWN

So there I sit, uneasy and languid, and Harriet makes her announcement. She gets up from the table and, without saying a word, she motions me into the kitchen. When I get to where the cabinets are, Harriet starts taking things out of one of them and handing them to me: Gussie's brass candlesticks she used to light Friday night candles and, esoterically, in her healings. I hadn't seen them since Gussie had died. Gussie's glass she used to use—the one with the red, white and black bands on it—to read the tea leaves and the salt. As she hands them to me, Harriet instructs me to place them on the kitchen table where my parents are waiting. Harriet and I sit back down and she announces that it's time, at that moment, to initiate me as the head of the family lineage; she explains that her mother, Gussie, had told her to do this. That really shocks me. Because no one had talked about Gussie or the healings, or the esoteric realities of Gussie and her family, since the day she died. And she had been dead seventeen years at that point. So, for seventeen years there had been no mention of this lineage, its healings, its teachings, or its obligations. It is as though none of it ever existed. And suddenly, I'm being initiated as head of a nonexistent, unmentionable lineage.

Harriet then proceeds to go into a trance and begins to transmit the teachings to me. It's the first transmission I'd received since Gussie died. And here I am. Sitting there. Receiving this wonderful transmission. Whatever Gussie had not imparted from the family lineage was being downloaded to me right then and there. So Harriet was actually the carrier, not the practitioner, of the family capacity. And, however long that transmission went on for, it really filled me up. I was already full from dinner and now I was full in an entirely different way.

My wife, who was part Native American and had spiritual training from a different tradition, was witnessing all this. She later told me that Harriet's actions made my parents very uncomfortable; they kept fidgeting and whispering to each other, and she said it looked like they couldn't wait for this to be over.

I have no idea how long the transmission went on. It was an event out of time. When it was over, my wife had to hang onto me physically; I was literally not capable of taking care of myself in that moment. I was disoriented and in some kind of shock. I don't remember much after that. I do remember waking up at home the next morning and asking my wife to tell me what she had witnessed. And sure enough, she had witnessed what I had experienced: After seventeen years of silence, I was being acknowledged as the student of my teacher and as her heir—just like she gifted me all those years ago in a Bronx maternity hospital. I understood that my teacher had been a student of her grandmother. In the transmission I was given I learned that it was a woman's lineage and the transmission was to go from Gussie to Harriet, but Harriet was not capable—so here I was. I was being gifted with a responsibility intended for women, for a lineage that was handed down between grandmother and granddaughter for generations. Even as a young woman in Central Europe. Gussie had known that the lineage must be preserved, but no female heir had been available. At least no female Gussie felt comfortable passing the teachings on to.

I knew all of that now. I had gotten some sense of the history. The capacities I was given became more apparent over time. Over years, actually.

The day after talking with my wife, I phoned my parents to ask them if they knew whether Harriet had planned the ceremony and, if they had been forewarned, why they hadn't mentioned it to me so I could have been more prepared. Both of my parents denied that there had been any so-called ceremony; they insisted that nothing out of the ordinary had occurred—just the usual family chatter and gossip. I tried talking to them about it a few more times, but they continued to insist that no initiation had ever taken place. And for them, it hadn't. For the rest of my mother's family, it hadn't. No one in the family, other than Harriet, had any interest whatsoever in what Harriet had done or who my grandmother was, or who her grandmother was. To them, it was all nonsense and story and fantasy. And, most importantly, it was un-American because Americans don't talk like that, they don't have contact with any of that kind of old country nonsense. It was doubly odd because my mother and her sisters all had the same esoteric powers as Gussie did—the lineage, as I mentioned, passed through the women in the family. But they chose to dismiss it. That's what happened to the esoteric healers who arrived here in the States from Central and Eastern Europe. Their children and grandchildren really had no interest in any of it. It wasn't American. And if there was no one to carry it forward it would just disappear. To this day there is no one in my family, an immense family of cousins and second cousins, their children and their children's children—no one who has ever expressed any interest in this lineage. When I die, the lineage will die with me; I am unable to pass it to anyone else because it's a family inheritance.

Teaching On My Own

After Gussie died, and before I reunited with Harry and Harriet, I continued to use the healing powers she had given me whenever I felt that there was a good reason to do so. I did have a consistent and focused practice of offering healings to Lucille and my children and stepdaughter. But beyond that, it was more of a spontaneous gesture. If I was with a friend, for example, or if I saw someone on the subway or on the street looking distressed, I would offer a healing.

I didn't really start a daily practice of healing others until I was in my early 40s—in the 1980s. It was then that I decided, on a whim, to move to Northern California. My sister lived there and offered to let me crash on her couch until I found a place to live; otherwise I knew no one and no one knew me. And yet, oddly enough, I hadn't been there long before people began seeking me out, asking for healings—as though they had been waiting for me. The requests kept coming. It felt like a déja vu moment from my childhood—sitting in Gussie's kitchen as she healed one visitor after another—except these people weren't Yiddish and they weren't all dressed in black. They weren't from the old country; these were New Agers and they spoke this funny New-Age language. So here I was, living in a community reminiscent of my grandmother's, where people are knocking at the door looking to be healed. But this time, they're looking for me. They don't come in silence, and they don't think they have an evil eye problem. But they do—they just have a different way of describing it.

After a while, I began to schedule the healings, creating a more formal structure of client-healer. People would phone for an appointment and, at the end of our time together, pay me for the healing. Their requests sometimes involved a physical illness, a debilitating disease, a difficult emotional problem, or a specific challenge they had with a friend, a partner, or their children. There were all sorts of requests for healings.

These healings were simply a continuation of what I had experienced with Gussie and what I had been doing informally since I was a very young student of hers. I knew I was ready and that I could sustain that kind of daily effort. I wasn't concerned about projecting onto people, distorting what was going on, or somehow misusing or depleting my gifts. I just believed that I was old enough and developed enough that I could trust myself to start a consistent daily practice of healings. And so I did—and I've been doing it ever since.

I healed my clients the way Gussie had taught me—through the eyes and always in silence. Because Gussie transmitted everything telepathically, I learned from a very young age to do the same. I learned to pay attention to what wanted to be known, to see what presented itself and to listen with all my faculties before offering an appropriate healing.

I did the best I could with each person who came to see me. And then, after a while, I began to sense that I didn't know enough and lacked some important skills. I didn't know what I meant by that, I just knew I needed more training. And I decided that training should be with a native or indigenous teacher, someone who came from an authentic tradition here in the Americas.

PART TWO

MY JOURNEY
TO PERU

Healing in the Andes

For my 50th birthday, the woman I was dating at the time suggested we go to Peru to celebrate. Sounded good to me even though I didn't know a thing about Peru, and frankly, had never been interested in learning. We should go to Cusco, she decided and I agreed. I knew even less about Cusco. What about Machu Picchu? We could go there, she said. Whatever. I had no clue what Machu Picchu even was. I was just up for going somewhere and I enjoyed her company. We had already traveled a bit together so I knew she had good ideas for places to go, places I knew nothing about. So, Peru it was.

We flew into Lima and then took one of these old, dilapidated airplanes to Cusco that felt like it was on its last legs. We had no trouble getting reservations anywhere once we got to Cusco since very few tourists were eager to visit back then.

WHAT WANTS TO BE KNOWN

The war was still raging between the Peruvian military, the official army of the Government; the Communist Party, better known as the Shining Path; and the Marxist guerrilla group Túpac Amaru Revolutionary Movement (MRTA), which made it much too dangerous for most people to visit the region.

We were fortunate to get booked into the Libertador Hotel, a converted mansion in the heart of the Old City that had been the home of a Spanish aristocrat who had settled in Cusco. It was what was called a traveler's hotel, as opposed to a tourist hotel. You could actually meet travelers on their way to and from their destination, and the hotel provided all sorts of services they might need. It had a place where you could leave your valuables—a room guarded 24/7 by the staff. You could put your passport and whatever else in a little box, lock it up and it was truly safe. You definitely didn't want to carry that stuff with you when you ventured into Cusco—there were a lot of desperate people who wanted what you had and would attack you to get it.

We loved staying there. There was a wood-burning fireplace in the elegant old lobby—quite unusual in Cusco, where there was little wood to burn. In fact, it was one of the only places in Cusco where you could sit next to a fire. So I would sit there in the old lobby and drink the coca tea they made, which helped with my altitude challenges. Cusco is 11,000 feet up and it was the highest place I had ever been. Coca tea really helped.

Anyway, the first night we were there, the woman I was dating announced that she had invited a man to join us for dinner, someone she had heard about through a friend of hers. So around 8 o'clock he walked into the dining room of the Libertador. He introduced himself as Juan Nuñez del Prado. He was graceful, if not elegant; dressed in rather unremarkable clothing, clothing that an educated man would wear in Cusco—conservative, nondescript, European. And he spoke fluent English with a slight Peruvian accent.

We learned, over the course of the evening, that he was an anthropologist who had worked at one of the local universities but was no longer teaching. He was out of work or between teaching assignments—I couldn't quite figure it out and never did learn what the story was. But it didn't matter. He was obviously looking for something to do, so he offered to show me around Cusco the next day and I enthusiastically agreed.

Early the next morning Juan arrived at the Libertador and we started out. We went directly to the Cathedral in Cusco for early morning Mass. I had never attended Mass before in a church, any church. This was a huge cathedral and, in a side chapel, I saw a life-sized black Christ nailed to a crucifix. Juan Nunez told me that it had been in that very spot since at least the mid-17th century. At any rate, there I was sitting in the Cathedral, tired, hungry and suffering from altitude sickness, when I began to experience an emanation from the black Christ. It was extraordinary. I was completely taken over by it. The Black Christ is a non-European, dark-skinned representation of Jesus Christ—of great significance to the Quechua people. It stands in sympathy with the oppressed and persecuted Quechua majority. I stood looking at it for a long time; then we left there and went on to various places in Cusco that were also of esoteric interest.

Although the Quechua were in the majority in Peru, they were incredibly persecuted. They weren't allowed in hotels or restaurants; they couldn't use the public bathrooms, own cars, or vote. They had no identity papers. They existed, according to the Peruvian government, merely as objects of tourist fascination. And since Cusco's economy was based on tourism, they had no choice but to tolerate the Quechua. To meet an educated Peruvian, like Juan Nuñez, who spoke Quechua was highly unusual. He was very much in his body, very grounded. His father was a prominent Peruvian anthropologist, famously known for his advocacy of the Quechua. Wherever Juan Nuñez went, people recognized him as the son of the famous man who had advocated for Quechua, which meant he enjoyed access to both worlds.

Juan Nuñez was more than an academic. He was also a student of a Quechua Indian, a priest by the name of don Benito Qoriwaman, the same

PART TWO: MY JOURNEY TO PERU

don Benito Shirley MacLaine had met on her first trip to Cusco and Machu Picchu and written about in one of her books. Juan and another student, Américo Eibar, had trained as a team with don Benito. I met Américo a few times; he and I did not have much of a rapport, but that didn't matter. Juan and I did and I thoroughly enjoyed the four or five days we spent together on that first visit.

A few weeks after Juan and I were at the Cathedral, I had an experience that seemed quite real at the time, but in retrospect, was clearly a vision of the black Christ—and it gave me a blessing. It appeared to be an older version of the teenage Jesus of Nazareth that I had met years ago in a cave in India. I received blessings that day as well.

A month or so after my first trip, I returned to Cusco, alone. The woman I was dating wasn't the least bit interested in returning to Peru and wanted nothing further to do with the Andes. I spent about ten days with Juan Nuñez, traveling and visiting villages and towns in and around Cusco. It became obvious to me really quickly that once you leave Cusco, the countryside is almost entirely populated by Quechua.

I spent about a year or so traveling back and forth between Northern California and Cusco. Each time, I would stay at the Libertador and arrange to be with Juan for a week to ten days. He loved to take me places and explain about the archaeology and the anthropological research he was doing, as well as the research his father had done. He often talked about the instruction don Benito had given him and what it was like to be don Benito's student. He was most generous with his time and his knowledge and I enjoyed our time together immensely.

On my third or fourth trip, I arrived at the Liberator Hotel fairly early in the morning and was enjoying my first cup of coca tea by the fire, grateful for the hotel's hospitality and the warmth of the fire. Suddenly, I became aware that someone was speaking to me in a heavily accented English. "Señor Goodberg?" I looked up to see two suits staring down at me.

"Will you please accompany us, Señor Goodberg?"

"Of course."

I stood up, relieved to see that they weren't interested in arresting me—at least not right away. They wanted me to accompany them somewhere, which I just assumed would be police headquarters. They turned around and walked toward the exit of the hotel. I put down my tea, got up, and followed them out onto the street, made a couple lefts, and entered an expensive, very modern tourist hotel, clearly made for people with big money. Our final destination was the dining room directly off the lobby. Sitting alone at a table, in a nearly empty dining room, was a rather elegantly dressed woman of maybe 40 or so. The suits walked right up to where she was seated, nodded to her and motioned for me to follow. She looked at me quickly and indicated with a sweep of her hand that I should sit next to her. She didn't say a word. The suits stood off to the side.

Then, staring straight ahead, she said, "My maid has given me the evil eye." Her English was flawless, with no trace of an accent. She said it again. "My maid has given me the evil eye. Please remove it at once." We were sitting, maybe a foot or two from each other, at a large round table. I moved my chair so that I could face her, and said, "of course." There was a lot of negativity in her and surrounding her. I cleared her of all that; I simply removed it. She felt so relieved. She sat there for quite a while and finally said, "Thank you. I am in your debt. My husband is the president of the Peruvian Senate. If you ever need anything, get in touch with him directly," and she handed me his card.

No sooner had she done that then the suits were at my side. "Please, Señor, follow us." I stood up, bowed slightly to her, and followed them out of the hotel, onto the street, into the Libertador, and back to my chair in front of the fire where I had been when they found me. Without saying another word, they were gone. I picked up my tea, but of course it was cold. I drank it anyway.

Another time, Juan Nuñez suggested we go to Machu Picchu so I could practice my healing skills in the middle of the tumultuous tourist crowd. We barely got inside the gates, when I was approached by a Quechua man, who looked to be in his mid-30s. He stepped right in front of me and started talking and I had no idea who he was or what he was saying. Juan Nuñez translated, explaining that this man had injured his leg in a farming accident when it became entangled in a piece of machinery. Although his leg had healed as best it could, it was still pretty messed up, causing him to walk with a noticeable limp and a great deal of pain. He asked if I could fix his leg so that he could walk normally again. I was surprised by his request. How did he know I could do that? I hadn't done much healing at all in the Andes—just that woman at the hotel. Nonetheless, I asked Juan to tell the man to come to our hotel in Machu Picchu that evening. There was only one hotel back then, which was immediately adjacent to the entrance to the archaeological zone. It was an inexpensive, occasionally had hot water, and consistently served very bad food.

That evening, he appeared at my door. I had no idea how he found me, but, sure enough, when I opened the door, he was standing right there. I invited him in, of course, but he was obviously uncomfortable. It was quite clear he had never been in a hotel; and he had certainly never been in a hotel room or anywhere, for that matter, with a European.

He stood in the middle of the room and waited for his healing.

I remember standing opposite him. I never

asked him to show me his leg. I never asked him anything. I simply offered a healing for him, as best I could. After some time, the healing was over and he turned around and left. He didn't thank me, he didn't offer a gift in return; he just left. We stayed at Machu Picchu a few more days, Juan Nuñez and I. The reciprocal gift, of course, was that I never again had to pay admission at the gate. Somehow whoever was there always knew who I was.

A few months later, Juan Nuñez and I were back at Machu Picchu. As we walked up to the gate, one of the men standing nearby approached me. I recognized him right away. It was the man whose leg I had attempted to heal and he had a big smile on his face. He couldn't wait to walk into the archaeological zone with us so he could show us that he no longer had a limp. He was walking normally and easily. I didn't ask to see his leg; it was clear to me that whatever I had done had restored his capacity to walk normally.

I remember another time when I was at the home of a guide and wrangler Juan Nuñez knew, the guide we used to take us deeper into the Andes, beyond Cusco. His house was at the end of a road and at the beginning of the horse trail. This particular afternoon, as we were getting ready to leave, his wife walked outside. She was quite bent over and couldn't stand up straight.

Our guide told us that his wife had been suffering for years. He looked directly at me and asked if I would heal his wife so that she would no longer be in pain and could stand straight. I remember standing there looking at them both, not the least bit convinced that I could be of help. But I didn't want to say no to him, so I stood opposite her and offered her a healing as best I could.

We returned to our guide's home more than a week later. As we were preparing to meet our vehicle for the ride back to Cusco, his wife came out to greet us. She was standing completely upright! We all just stood there and stared at her, no one more amazed than I was. She told us, in Quechua, that she was no longer in pain, and had no trouble standing or walking. She felt entirely healed of whatever had been bothering her. Over the next year or two, I saw them both fairly frequently and became an honored guest at their home. She was always standing erect and often marveled at how good she felt. I had no clue how any of this had happened. I had no way of explaining how a man with a damaged leg who could walk again easily and normally. I had no way of explaining how this woman could be pain free.

Every now and then, the healings were dramatic transformations. I offered dozens and dozens of healings in the villages on the way to and from Chua Chua. Many times I succeeded. And many times I didn't. But I almost always brought some kind of relief, some sense of peace and comfort.

I was always invited to dine with the family afterwards; we would sit together on the floor around a common pot of soup. There were some days when I'd offer as many as five healings in the village, which meant that I had to eat five full meals. So, by the end of all that, I felt really quite ill—overly stuffed and suffering. I had eaten too much, and none of it had agreed with me. In these villages almost everyone was malnourished and food was incredibly sparse. So, to invite someone to dine was a real act of generosity and, of course, I was expected to eat whatever was offered. I did my best.

Interestingly enough, the healings that I gave to the Quechua people were always easier to do than those I provided to Westerners. That puzzled me for a long time. Why was I so much more effective with Quechua than I was with Westerners? It's not that I was unsuccessful with Westerners—quite to the contrary. I continue to offer successful healings to Westerners, but never quite as easily as with Quechua.

I came to understand that the Quechua have a greater capacity to receive and use the gifts I was offering. They had an intuitive sense of how to receive a healing and how to allow it to do whatever it needed to do to work. This innate capacity to receive, to use the healing, is part of our species wisdom. This capacity is hardwired within us. Natural healings from healers have continued uninterrupted for thousands and thousands of years in the Andes, but not so in the West. Instead, we turn to medical interventions and so-called alternative healings, and we've forgotten how to respond to a natural healer.

In order for my healing to be effective with a Westerner, I realized that I needed to reawaken the individual's capacity to receive and use the healing.

What Took You So Long?

During my time with Juan Nuñez, he spoke often about his experiences with his teacher, don Benito, the instructions he had received, and the experiences he had had upon completing his studies. By then, don Benito had died. At some point, Juan began to talk about his current teacher, a man who lived a traditional life in the remote village of Chua Chua, in a region called Q'eros, which was even more remote. He often made journeys back and forth to visit with his teacher. At that point, my time with Juan Nuñez was coming to an end. I didn't think there was much more I could learn from him or many more places he could take me to. We had pretty much covered his map.

But then, one day, Juan said to me, "Would you like to go to the religious festival at Quyllur Rit'i next month?" This festival, he explained, had been happening yearly, for at least a thousand years. It was a way for the Quechua to pay homage to Ausungate, a mountain very sacred to them, and to the Christian God, who was represented by the little church in the meadow—the spiritual center of the festival—which housed a sacred stone containing the energetic of Christ.

It would be unlike any other festival in the Andes, Juan said. First of all, there'd be no drinking or partying—it was a quiet, somber, and dignified gathering focused on spiritual pursuits. Secondly, it attracted between 50,000 and 60,000 Quechua, who'd be spending the week together in the bowl of a glacier. I would get to experience the Quechua as a group and witness how they express themselves spiritually. I was all for it. Besides, Juan added, it might be an opportunity for me to meet his teacher, don Manuel Quispe. Even better.

A month or so later, I returned to Cusco and we set out for Quyllur Rit'i, which proved to be quite the journey. Obviously we needed a jeep with four-wheel drive in order to navigate some pretty terrible terrain. And then, once we got to the end of the road, we had to abandon the jeep and continue on horseback, definitely a first for me. In fact, I was grateful to Juan for letting me know what to expect so that I could take riding lessons back in Northern California in anticipation of this journey.

It was my first time venturing beyond the world I had known. We were in the Quechua world. Completely off the grid. No cell phones or reliable

PART TWO: MY JOURNEY TO PERU

GPS, of course—it was the 90s after all. I spoke almost no Spanish, other than to ask where the bathroom was, and certainly no Quechua. Juan Nuñez spoke both, so he acted as my interpreter.

Juan hired a guide who became my guide, too. He was the one who supplied the horses and all the camping gear and made sure that I stayed safe in the midst of what was still a civil war. After a few days, we made it to the festival, which is to say we arrived at a big open meadow surrounded by glacial mountains, adjacent to Ausangate and swarming with thousands of Quechua. Everyone camped, of course, they just laid down and slept on the open meadow. Juan Nuñez and I shared a tent—and we even had a campfire the wrangler tended for us. That meant I could have a hot breakfast most days—a cup of coffee and maybe an egg or a little potato soup, depending on what was available.

Everyone, in this huge mass of people, was very polite, very sober, and very reverent, dressed traditionally. In my wanderings, I ran into a small group of Canadians, the only other non-native people there, whom I spent a little time with. They had hired an outfitter who set up three or four tents for them and brought a camp chef with them. They even had a portable bathroom I could use occasionally—the only bathroom in the whole meadow.

Quyllur Rit'i was organized by region and village. Each village brought their own band along—

a half dozen or more musicians who played music representative of their community. All these bands marched in an oval around the little church that housed the sacred stone, so at any one time there might be fifteen to twenty village bands, each playing a different song, using mostly trumpets and drums, with an occasional flute or pair of cymbals thrown in. And they played 24/7. The music and the dissonance never stopped, it never got softer, it just kept going. When a band got tired, another band took over. To get into the church, you had to find an opening between the bands and slip through. So there was constant noise and then, of course, it rained, it snowed, it dipped below freezing every night. The meadow turned to a sea of mud and, with no bathrooms, it turned into a sea of muck.

When it got cold, after the sun went down, it was much easier to walk, except for the fact that it was entirely dark and no one owned a flashlight. On clear nights, the sky was very bright, but that didn't happen often. Most nights were clouded and fogged over. So the meadow was very dark and very crowded with no street patterns marked off except one main walkway that ran through the middle of the camp. You were always walking into people who were sitting or standing or lying down; once you stepped off that main walkway, you were in a sea of people.

Two days into our stay there, I got altitude sickness. I was nauseous, headachy, and had massive diarrhea. On top of all that, I was cold, hungry, and awash in mud. I'd been walking in mud, my tent was full of mud and kept collapsing under the weight of mud. It was right around that time that Juan Nuñez suggested that I meet don Manuel.

I didn't pay much attention to his invitation; I was too overwhelmed. I was in sensory, and mud, overload. So I just, "Sure, I'd like to meet don Manuel." And then, Juan Nuñez issued his caveat, "Just so you know, he hates Europeans. He's never talked to one. Don't expect him to acknowledge you or want to meet with you or spend any time with you. I wanted to say, "So, why are you introducing me?" But I didn't. I just nodded and said, "I'd be happy to meet your teacher."

Somehow we found our way through this sea of people and got onto this one walkway where no one was sitting or lying down and we could walk the entire length of the camp. We got to the other side of the camp—away from where my tent was—and I noticed a group of maybe fifteen or twenty people, somehow set apart from the hordes. They were all sitting together, dressed in traditional dress, very quiet. It was obvious they hadn't brought their own village band, they had no music with them. They were just sitting there quietly. We stopped directly in front of them.

I stood there as Juan Nuñez walked into the group; it was obvious that he knew them and that they were people from the remote region of Q'eros, the people his father had advocated for. I watched as Juan Nuñez stopped next to an older man, whom I hadn't noticed at first. He was small. He was old. He was hidden, seemingly surrounded by members of the group, and Juan was talking to him. The man didn't seem to be paying any attention to what Juan was saying, but after a while, Juan came back and said, "Don Manuel wants to meet you at your tent."

"My tent? How does he know I have a tent? How does he know where it is? How is he going to find it? How am I going to find it? Can you help me?"

We somehow got back to my tent, I had no idea how.

By the time we arrived, a tiny little man was already there waiting for me. I figured he must be don Manuel. I hadn't been able to see him very clearly before, but up close I could see who he was. I was a giant compared to him—and I'm quite short myself! Anyway, he was waiting and when I walked up to him, he turned and walked into the tent without bending over. I followed him. I had my boots on and he was wearing sandals cut out from old tires. All I could think of was, god, we are tracking more mud into the tent—and god, that guy is short.

It was dark in the tent. Don Manuel started talking right away in Quechua; he kept on talking and I couldn't tell if he was speaking to me or chanting or praying. I didn't know what he was doing. We stood facing each other and this went on for what seemed like forever. And then, suddenly, he stopped talking, walked behind me and stood there. I immediately felt a stunning blow between my upper shoulder blades. A sharp, sudden blow. It nearly knocked me over. At that moment the material world seemed to lose all significance and my senses became acutely tuned to the energetic emanations I was swimming in. This sense of swimming or floating in an endlessness of energies only seemed to intensify during the remainder of the festival.

It was that moment, the moment he struck my back, that I've never been able to adequately explain, or understand, or even fully describe. All I can say is that, from that moment on, my life took on an entirely different quality. It's a before and after....before that moment and after that moment.

I stood there a little while longer and then walked out of the tent. Don Manuel followed suit. Don Manuel started speaking again in a more conversational tone, looking directly at me. I asked Juan Nuñez to tell me what don Manuel was saying. He told me that don Manuel wanted to know what took me so long to show up. He had gotten tired of waiting for me.

Suddenly I felt as though I was playing a part in a B-movie. I couldn't imagine why this guy had been expecting me or what he had been waiting for exactly. Was this some kind of a hoax or some kind of an in-joke that I wasn't privy to? Was I replaying a scene in a Carlos Castaneda book? I snapped back to attention just as Juan was saying, "And he wants you to accompany him back to his village. Now."

"What? Right now? Where does he live? How far away is it? How is he getting there?"

"He walked here with other villagers and it'll take about a week to walk back over some very high passes. They sleep on the trail and they eat whatever is available. He wants you to accompany him."

I realized that this guy actually had been waiting for me and apparently wanted to teach me right away. I had no idea what he wanted to teach me, no idea what he was offering. I really knew nothing about him.

I remember saying to Juan Nuñez, "Tell don Manuel that I will join him at his village in six weeks. I must go home. But I will be there in six weeks."

Juan Nuñez conveyed that to don Manuel, who turned around and left. Didn't say goodbye, just left; I remained outside the tent with Juan.

I spent the rest of the week wandering around by myself, feeling somehow that chronological time and personal events had been fractured after that blow between the shoulder blades. They fractured even further soon after I ran into Juan Nuñez, who had arranged for me to enter the little church, step behind a rope barrier—even though no Europeans had ever been allowed to— and touch the sacred rock with its mysterious image of Jesus at the altar.

In my meanderings, I managed to find my way back to my tent a few times—it had completely collapsed in the mud—and I even shared a meal or two with the Canadians at their camp. At some point, the people at the festival started to leave, so I left with them. I remember massive numbers of us walking down to a dirt road; I remember getting onto the back of a stake truck with a whole group of Quechua. We all piled on, standing shoulder to shoulder, and took off down the road.

At some point that evening I had to go to the bathroom. The truck stopped for a moment so I could relieve myself. Instead of getting back on the truck, I lay down on the side of the road and went to sleep. The next morning I got up and flagged down another truck. It stopped and we continued on until we arrived back in Cusco. I have no idea how I made it back to the Libertador Hotel. I was cold, hungry, exhausted, and filthy—and the altitude was making me sick. I had lost all the gear and clothing I had taken with me; I had on what I had been wearing in my wanderings at the festival.

For some reason the hotel wasn't expecting me for another day or two, and they were entirely booked. The Easter Festival was happening in Cusco, so they had no rooms available. One of the managers decided to put me up for the night in his office, which had a couch that converted into a bed and it had a bathroom. Fortunately, I had extra clothing in a locker at the Libertador. They even brought me a meal. I slept well, but the next day when I awoke, I was completely incoherent, swimming in a confusion of energetic emanations. Nothing that came out of my mouth made sense. Nothing in my surroundings made sense. I couldn't seem to function at all.

That afternoon, Juan Nuñez showed up at the hotel to make sure that I could get on a flight back to the States. I had lost my initial reservation because I hadn't called to confirm or reconfirm; there certainly weren't any telephones at the festival to call 48 hours in advance. So, Juan and I went to see someone who arranged for me to get another flight out. Luckily, I had done this journey so many times that I could pretty much be on auto-pilot, because I have no idea how I got to the airport or got on the plane. I have no idea how I managed to change planes at Lima and again at Miami, disembark in San Francisco, and find a taxi to take me back to my apartment in Sausalito. I was incoherent, sick, and barely able to function. I remained that way for the next few weeks. Truthfully, I don't remember anything from those weeks— they're just gone.

It took about three weeks before I was able to pay attention to anything. Shortly after that, I was on my way back to Cusco to meet Juan Nuñez and the wrangler, who had agreed to accompany me to Chua Chua for my first encounter with don Manuel on his home turf. Chua Chua, as I mentioned, was still quite remote in the early 90s, only reachable by horseback. But we made it, and just as I promised, six weeks after meeting don Manuel, I arrived at his home and he was there to meet me. It was then that I started my formal studies with him.

BECOMING FEARLESS

When I agreed to be don Manuel's student, I understood him to be a shaman and the carrier of an ancient Incan wisdom. So I thought my challenge was to learn a system of ritual magic and recover an imperial wisdom. The magical system would help me be more effective with relieving personal suffering and the Incan wisdom would somehow 'empower' me. That turned out to be only partly true. Yes, don Manuel taught me traditional ritual magic and no, he was not a carrier of the high culture of the Inca elite. Quietly, he practiced an esoteric technology for healing the Q'eros region and he gifted me with the esoteric wisdom and technologies of his lineage, most of which he did not personally practice.

When I first arrived at his home, don Manuel helped clear an area near his house for my tent and camp. After dinner, he gave a despacho, a magical offering to the mountain gods. He then asked what I wanted. I sensed it was a test question so I replied that I wanted a full teaching. He responded by energetically "cleansing" me with his mesa, his ritual magic "bundle." He opened up his mesa and took out a small, dark sculpted rock, which he then rubbed on my upper body in a sequence he repeated at other times during my first few visits to Chua Chua. The only things inside his mesa were a dozen or so small rocks and a few small child's trinkets, which I later learned wasn't all that surprising. An esoteric master can transform ordinary objects into extraordinary tools for ritual magic.

Our evenings soon took on a regular pattern: I would join don Manuel for dinner with his family, followed by a despacho, and then a long period of silence that usually ended around daylight. During the despacho, his nightly prayer offering, I usually turned on a flashlight, so I could see the arrangement of the cocoa leaves and all the various items that were laid out in a very specific order, on a large piece of paper spread out in front of him. Manuel must have shown me a couple hundred different arrangements of leaves and other items. Each constituted a particular offering with a particular purpose.

He wanted me to see all of these despachos, to experience each of them, which is to say to absorb the energetic or instructional gift contained within the structure and process of each despacho. These despachos were expressions of devotion and were created with an extraordinary reverence.

Often a despacho was a request for healing or kindness from the Andes, which the Andeans considered sacred. The most sacred of these mountains had particular capacities for healing and gifting. So a despacho would be a request for a healing or gift, perhaps someone ill, an animal who was ill, a child who was ill, crops that needed help. There were all sorts of requests that these sacred mountains could respond to.

Manuel was particularly connected to Ausangate, the mountain adjacent to the Qoyllur Rit'i festival, where I had met him. After a despacho was completed and he lingered over it for a while, he wrapped it up in the paper it was made on and put it aside, to be burned the next day over a dung fire. After the despacho was wrapped up and put aside, we sat in silence, for several hours. We never slept, although I would sometimes doze off.

These periods of silence were not meditations. Rather, they were occasions for don Manuel to gift me with the esoteric wisdom of his lineage. These gifts were non-verbal or telepathic communications of great intensity, which penetrated my awareness even when I dozed off in the darkness and chill of don Manuel's unheated home. During these extended late night silences, I struggled with altitude sickness, mostly headaches and nausea, intestinal distress brought on by the local food and water, and the ever present fleas. These distractions were a frequent source of self-doubt. Was I too ill to retaining the unspoken teachings? Finally, I became too weak from dehydration to continue and reluctantly announced my departure from Chua Chua with a promise to return shortly.

I was always aware of receiving don Manuel's transmissions, a gifting that had no words. My awareness was body-based; it was a somatic awareness. I felt as though my whole body were being fed. It was completely dark and we had no clocks or watches available, but as far as I could tell, each transmission would last anywhere from a half hour to an hour. So we'd sit there in silence in the dark until Manuel announced that it was time for a ceremony—a nightly expression of devotion to the Virgin. Don Manuel belonged to a cult of the Virgin, an adoration cult, which best as I could tell was based at the Cathedral in Cusco.

Spoken entirely in Quechua, with Spanish words sprinkled in for the Virgin, Mother Mary, and the Mother of God, Don Manuel's nightly expression had a predictable uniformity to it. He would bring out two wine glasses and a bottle of something that might be whiskey, which I had brought him from Cusco, or it might be the colorless white liquid made from potatoes, something like a vodka or, what we used to call White Lightening in the States. I refused to drink what was offered to me—it was much too strong—and at high altitude and with my altitude illness and intestinal issues, I was really unwilling to drink to the Virgin.

WHAT WANTS TO BE KNOWN

So most nights he and I had a bit of a tussle, a bit of conflict when I turned down his offer. I would raise my glass, put it to my lips, let the alcohol touch my lips and then put the glass down. At some point he would drink my glass too and the ceremony would be complete. Don Manuel conducted this adoration of the Virgin, as both a cult member and as an Andean High Priest. He wore both hats and I came to realize that the figures of the Christ, the Christ Child, the Virgin, John the Baptist, had all been folded into the Andean point of view. So Manuel was a Christian in the sense that Andeans were Christians—he absorbed the gods of another religion. The Andean religion was seemingly able—or should I say, flexible, fluid, or open enough—to absorb an infinite number of these Christian gods.

After the ceremony, we'd return to silence and he'd resume his transmission. It was a full meal, this generous gifting. It had no content that I could recognize cognitively, but I knew for certain that I was being gifted with an ongoing download of wisdom and capacities.

Death and my fear of death, my fear of the fear of death and my fear of heights all accompanied me to Peru. In the early '90s, Lima had plague, cholera, and car bombs; visitors were routinely instructed to stay away from hotel windows. Cusco had military, police, and insurgent violence. Alone at night in hotels in Cusco and Lima, anxiety and fear would visit me.

PART TWO: MY JOURNEY TO PERU

Don Manuel made a decision early on in my training that I would be free of fear or I would die. So late one night—perhaps an hour or two before dawn when the Andes were at their coldest, the wind was up and the fog was in—he stood up, motioned to me to follow, and walked rapidly into the cold and foggy darkness. I managed to make my way through his house without tripping on anything or waking any of the family, and hustled to catch up with him, careful not to step in any of the dung, which was all over the village. I was also concerned that I might have an unwelcome nocturnal encounter with a drunk villager because once night fell most of them would start to drink and end up stumbling around in the dark.

Anyway, by the time we left the house, it was quite late—around three or four in the morning. I was tired and cold, headachy and nauseous from altitude sickness, and I couldn't see very well because the fog had covered up the moon. Manuel kept a blistering pace, at least for me at that altitude, and I struggled to keep up with him. The high altitude clothing I was wearing back then didn't breathe at all. I chose it because I wanted to be protected against the elements—the moisture and the fog. Unfortunately, inside the gear, I was just as wet with sweat from exertion.

As soon as we left the village, I realized we were headed for a walk on one of the very narrow Andean trails that hugged the mountain's edge. I was petrified that I'd lose sight of Don Manuel and become lost in the Andean mountains forever, and that no one would come looking for me. My fear increased as the realization set in that we'd be walking in total darkness on slippery stones, on the edge of cliffs, ascending and descending at a rapid pace. I made every effort to maintain my balance and my equilibrium and not let my fear and anxiety paralyze me. I never knew how long these walks would go on—sometimes a half hour, other times maybe an hour. They seemed like an eternity.

I never did lose sight of don Manuel as he walked ahead of me, nor did I ever slip off the edge, twist an ankle, or break a bone. Nonetheless, as soon as we returned to don Manuel's house and sat down at our assigned places on the floor in the ceremonial area of his hut, I would breathe a big sigh of relief that the walk was over. Even though don Manuel resumed his teaching of me, I remained soaked in sweat, concerned about hypothermia and still struggling to calm down. Luckily, since I had, with Manuel's permission obviously, merged into him, I didn't need to be actively open to him. I was part of him, and whatever he was offering would simply come to me. There was no way to avoid it. However, in my anxiety and fear and panic I forgot I wasn't separate from him and I began to doubt my capacity to absorb what he was offering me. In truth, I absorbed all of it, because it was simply a matter of his willingness to be generous. It wasn't possible for me to resist it, because I had no separate existence. Spiritually, vibrationally, I was one with him.

This routine would go on for probably an hour or two after we returned from the nightly death walk and then he would indicate that it was time for me to leave. I would get up and stumble out the door, trying to stay awake, watching that I didn't run into a drunk villager, trying to avoid the dung and hoping I could find my tent and that it was still standing and I could get into my sleeping bag and go to sleep. And that my sleeping bag wasn't too wet from all the damn fog to sleep in.

More often than not, dawn had broken by the time I got back to my tent. I would take off my boots and my wet clothing, get into my sleeping bag and fall asleep immediately. Some hours later, I would wake. Village noises would wake me, kids playing, animal noises, people talking quietly, and the sun heating up the tent. It would become hot in the tent, so hot that I was unable to continue to sleep. The noises and the heat really did drive me out of the tent, into the bright Andean daylight.

Hopefully someone in my camp had made coffee or would make coffee, not an easy chore at that altitude. If I could just get a cup of coffee, maybe that would help with my headache and my tiredness because I could have slept another five or six hours. So my day began hopefully with the coffee, maybe something to eat, if I was lucky. Occasionally there'd be an egg gifted by or traded from a village family; maybe a potato to eat—

there wasn't much. My time in Chua Chua took its toll on my health. Each week I would lose three to five pounds, sometimes more, and after awhile I really started to look quite emaciated—because I was quite emaciated.

These death walks continued nightly. I must have gone on 40 or 50 of them, maybe more, I don't know. At the time all that mattered was that I didn't get lost or injured—I was even too frightened to think about dying. And then one night, when we returned to Don Manuel's house, I realized I had been on a walk without fear. I had been cautious, careful and soaked with sweat from the exertion, just like always, but my fears had lifted, like a high fever that had broken in the night. A burden was gone, a burden I had carried throughout my life. By the time we were back at his house, sitting on our rugs in his ceremonial area, I knew I had conquered my fear of these death walks and that this teaching was over. We didn't speak about what had happened, but we never went on another night walk. I had lost my fear and without fear, Manuel could then proceed to a different type of teaching. I was no longer the gringo novice. I was now fearless and capable of receiving what was next.

On a full moon after my fear died, I stood outside Don Manuel's house and listened as he explained the significance of that moon. I recall the intense brightness of that night in an unusually cloudless, fogless, high altitude sky. Don Manuel's announcement, which was translated for me, declared that this moon signaled the start of a new time. What was new was not specified but the emphasis was on new beginning and new. Nothing else seemed important in this short speech other than the implication that Don Manuel's lineage had a function to perform in the 'new time.'

As I write this now, I recall no sense of this 'new time' as anything other than another mythic story even if the storyteller was don Manuel. I had been listening to gossip, which was current at that time in the Andes, about the return of the Inca, the return of the Christ and the 'harmonic convergence.' But I imagined a 'new time' might be referring to externals like "regime change" or material prosperity for everyone. Much later, I understood that don Manuel was announcing a transformation within the higher or upper realms of the Sacred, a transformation whose impact on the material realm might not be readily obvious.

That night, I failed to grasp why don Manuel was announcing this "new time" to me. This was the first of only two speeches Don Manuel addressed to me that should have signaled that I was obligated to assist in the beginnings of this 'new time.' My life would become a devotion to bringing about this 'new time.'

My Training Comes to an End

I spent time with don Manuel every six weeks or so for I don't know how long—a couple years I think; maybe less, maybe more. I'd stay at his home in Chua Chua for about a week to ten days, depending on how I was feeling. The whole experience was taking a tremendous toll on my health; I struggled with pretty severe intestinal problems—chronic diarrhea, cramping, and dehydration—which caused my weight to plummet from my normal 150–155 pounds down to 125–130. At 125, I looked emaciated and I felt terrible. The altitude up at don Manuel's was insanely high (more than 14,500 feet), which added intense headaches, nausea and fatigue to my health woes.

I was really struggling financially as well. Before I met don Manuel, I was living comfortably enough—even though I didn't have any savings to speak of. But once I started commuting back and forth between the Bay Area and Chua Chua, I found myself increasingly unable to earn a living and was forced to finance my life on credit. By the time I stopped going to don Manuel's, I had maxed out all of my credit cards. I was really broke. Luckily, it was still possible to live quite cheaply in the Bay Area, so I was able to keep paying rent.

The civil war between the Shining Path and the Peruvian military was still raging and it was a difficult time for everyone—especially for the Quechua. The Quechua people suffered terribly from the brutal treatment they received from both sides. It was indeed a perilous time to be in Peru. I was fortunate that my trips to the Andes from Cusco to Chua Chua were facilitated by Carmen Arróspide, a young travel agent who handled the in-country logistics, including my stays at the Libertador Hotel, and Juan Nuñez, who handled the actual journeys and functioned as my interpreter and troubleshooter. Once we left Cusco, there were all kinds of potentially awful situations that he was able to cope with in ways that were not destructive to anyone.

When we went to Chua Chua, we traveled by jeep over really bad roads until we got to a village where the road ended and we had to continue on horseback. The horses were organized and cared for by a horse wrangler and guide, whose name I've forgotten (I'll call him don C). He always invited Juan Nuñez and me to stay the night at his home, a small house made of dried clay, in this remote village. I slept on the floor, in one of the rooms. The animals lived inside in the interior courtyard at night to protect them from thieves.

We'd set out from don C's home with our camping gear, our tents, and a few kilos of coca leaves as gifts. I chewed coca leaves the whole time—going to Chua Chua, being in Chua Chua, and returning to Cusco. Coca leaves really helped me. They helped everyone. As a mild euphoric, they curbed hunger and thinned the blood, which was helpful at high altitudes. We also brought medical supplies and some store-bought liquor for don Manuel. We had food for us and food for the horses. We had amassed quite a large group. There was the lead guide, a Quechua who selected our particular route and kept a look out for military patrols and Shining Path patrols; there was don C sitting on an Andean pony, Juan Nuñez on an Andean pony, and I on an Andean pony; and there were three or four Andean ponies serving as pack horses.

The small Andean ponies were quite docile. Thankfully, all I had to do was to sit on my pony, who would follow the pony in front of him. Don C was a Quechua dressed in European clothing; a well known man of good repute, kind and gentle and, although he only spoke Quechua and Spanish—and I only spoke English—he was always able to communicate with me. He looked after the horses and the gear, helped us set up camp, and cooked our meals. As soon as we'd get to Chua Chua, he'd pitch a tent for me and Juan and set up camp, always adjacent to don Manuel's house.

One journey, about a year and a half into my time as a guest at don Manuel's home, stands out as particularly interesting. I had been there for about a week or so and we had only a few more days together before I headed home. In the middle of the afternoon, one of don Manuel's sons came to me and said that his father wanted to meet with me right away, which was highly unusual. We never met before evening, when I would receive an invitation to dine with his family. And even then, I'd occasionally, have to wait while don Manuel met with a villager who came to see him for healing or who asked for coca leaf readings, in hopes of finding a lost animal.

This time it wasn't even close to dinner and I was quite perplexed. Nonetheless, I followed his son back to the house, took up my seat on the animal rug, and waited. It was warm in the house and dark, even in the middle of the afternoon. After awhile, don Manuel came in and took his usual seat across from me and there we remained, in complete silence. Before long, I began to receive a transmission that was unfamiliar and rather startling. It took on the potency of my first visit with don Manuel, when he came to my tent at the Quyllur Rit'i festival and smashed me on the back between the shoulder blades. Which is to say, it was an overwhelmingly powerful transmission.

WHAT WANTS TO BE KNOWN

I lost track of any sense of what was going on—even more so than usual. And, even more than usual, the whole experience took on an intensely dreamlike quality. I felt as though I were floating and yet I knew that I was quite Earth anchored. My being had become larger and had merged with don Manuel, which caused his being to become larger, too. I have no idea how long we sat there, but at some point we got up and walked outside, where a small crowd had gathered. Don Manuel's two sons, his daughter-in-law and grandkids, don C, the horse wrangler, Juan Nuñez and several villagers were all there. I was only vaguely aware of the crowd and remember thinking it was rather odd that they seemed to be waiting for us. The sun was bright and very strong and, of course, no one wore sunglasses, including me.

I remember standing there, facing don Manuel as his gifting continued, even stronger than before. It was almost too much to bear; I felt disoriented and was pretty sure I was going to pass out or fall over. And then at some point he walked up to me, kissed me and held me close to him. He had never kissed or held me before and nor did he ever do either again. He stepped back, looked straight at me and began to talk, indicating to Juan Nuñez that he wanted him to translate. I can't remember anything Manuel said. I just stood there, tottering, somehow managing not to collapse in a heap. I remember don Manuel smiling at me. I had never seen that kind—or any other kind—of smile on his face before; but there he was beaming.

When he finished his speech, he turned around and walked back in the hut. Everyone walked away and I was left standing there with Juan Nuñez. We walked around the side of the house for privacy. Juan Nuñez seemed agitated and annoyed.

"What did don Manuel say?" I wanted to know.

He didn't answer, so I asked him again. "What did he say?"

"He has declared you his peer."

I looked at him. "What does that mean? I don't understand what's going on."

"He has declared that he has finished teaching you and you are now an Andean High Priest and his peer."

And with that, Juan Nunez walked away, leaving me there in the bright sun, struggling to stay upright and trying to somehow make sense of what had just happened.

I don't remember what happened next. I must have had supper with the family as usual. I do know that I didn't spend the evening afterwards with don Manuel. I went right to my tent and fell asleep. The next day we struck camp and I said goodbye to everyone. Don Manuel was smiling warmly at me again, and I noticed that every one else had a different attitude toward me. Different from the day before. I was now someone of note, someone of prestige, someone of significance in that context, in that village, in that Q'eros region. And I was to be treated with respect and deference.

Unfortunately, my new status caused my relationship with Juan Nuñez to deteriorate rapidly. He was angry with me and even at times hostile, which made the trip back to Cusco quite unpleasant. I returned to the Liberator, stunned and confused by what had taken place with don Manuel. It was over and I was on my own. I felt isolated. I had no way to maintain contact with don Manuel. No way to phone him or send him a letter or visit with him. I knew he wanted his teachings brought to the West; I knew he wanted an Andean high priest to live in the West for that purpose; and I knew he had designated me as the high priest who would make that happen. Now I just needed somehow to figure out how to do all of that.

I seriously have no idea how I managed to get on a plane to Lima, fly to Miami, transfer to San Francisco, hail a taxi to Sausalito and let myself into my apartment. I sleepwalked through the first few weeks after I got home. It's still all a blur. What I do know is that I simply felt alone, isolated, confused, and unhappy. And immensely grateful to don Manuel. I remain to this day grateful to don Manuel.

One Last Time

Back home in Sausalito, as much as I missed being with don Manuel, I was relieved not to have to endure the high altitude, drink the water or eat the food, all of which conspired to make me ill with chronic intestinal distress for two or three years, which occasionally recurred for another five years or so. I needed time to recover my health and to regain the weight I had lost.

Just about the time I started feeling better, I began to sense that my time with don Manuel was incomplete. It became clear that I needed to visit him one more time; that there was something he had yet to give me. I knew I had to start making preparations to return to Cusco and then make my way back to Chua Chua. And I knew that I had to make the trip—my final journey—without Juan Nuñez. I only hoped that don C, the wrangler who had supplied the horses and camping gear and always looked after us, watching out for the military and Shining Path patrols, would be available when I arrived. Sadly, he wasn't; but he offered to have his son accompany us, along with enough horses for our gear and a lead guide. We didn't have an interpreter, so I asked Carmen Arróspide, the woman who had handled the logistics of my travels in Peru, to come along. I must say it took a while to convince her.

Carmen was in her mid-twenties at the time. Her mother was Quechua and she herself spoke fluent Quechua, along with several other languages, including Italian, German, and English. Carmen had a university degree in civil engineering but since no opportunities existed for women civil engineers in Cusco, she had taken a job in the tourist industry. Carmen wasn't all that keen on accompanying us. She had never ridden a horse before, she was concerned about the turmoil still present in rural areas, and she worried about the difficulties she'd be facing as a woman camping and eating and sleeping in such a remote village. Nonetheless, she was a good sport.

When we set out that first morning the weather was mild and pleasant. A typical spring day. And the weather remained like that for most of the trip. The afternoon before we entered the Q'eros region, however, things changed dramatically. As we headed up a high pass, the air was cool, dry, and clear—not a cloud in sight. But as we reached a wide open area near the summit, a storm appeared, without warning, out of nowhere, bringing with it snow, fierce winds, and freezing temperatures. We were not prepared. We had no rain gear, no warm clothes and no place to take shelter. Turning back wouldn't help us; all we could do was press forward. My fingers and toes were numb; my clothes were soaked through; I was chilled to the bone. Everyone else was in similar straits. I knew that the storm was potentially life threatening and if we tried to continue our ascent or turn back, we could potentially die from hypothermia.

Suddenly, I got it. I realized that this storm was a test; my final test from don Manuel. I knew I had to somehow stop the storm and restore the dry mild weather or else we would quite possibly freeze to death. There was nothing for it but to act. So, I created a large energetic wall, which I generated from my physicality, stretched it so that it became an enormous barrier, which I then could push forward into the oncoming storm. I pushed the storm back and back and back until it finally disappeared. We were once again in warm dry weather. The sun came back out and our gear (and our bodies) began to dry out.

As we finally crested the pass and descended toward Chua Chua. I wondered if I should reply in kind and threaten don Manuel's life. It quickly became clear to me that such an act would be foolish and disrespectful. I would simply ignore the incident, knowing full well that he was already aware that I had passed his final test. If he had any hesitation about gifting me any remaining capacities, that was all gone now and he was ready to give freely.

The dry weather lasted just long enough to get us to Chua Chua where it had begun to rain in earnest, turning the village into a sea of mud and churning up all kinds of animal droppings.

The mud was so deep that wherever I stepped I ran the risk of having the mud suck my boot right off my foot. So needless to say I found it impossible to walk and impossible to pitch a tent. Much to my surprise, Manuel offered his potato storage hut as a dry alternative for us to sleep in and he even helped clean it out. I gladly accepted his offer.

The potato storage hut was quite small and cramped, made worse by the fact that we were all sleeping there. And by the fact that don Manuel insisted on sleeping right next to me. I couldn't figure out why he would do that when we had never shared a common sleeping area before. But, he did. Each night he would lie down next to me and fall asleep immediately. And so would I. I slept incredibly soundly and each morning I woke up feeling oddly full, as if I had been filled up during the night, and yet I had no recall of anything happening.

Despite the nasty weather, don Manuel and I spent a lot of very pleasant time together. Our relationship had taken on a different quality. We were now peers and I was an honored guest. Each night we enjoyed each other's company and, as we sat across from one another in the dark, as we always had, he gave me some additional transmissions. After about a week, we said our good-byes and retraced our steps back to Cusco. I made my way back to the States soon afterwards.

I must say that I was grief stricken when I said my final good-bye to don Manuel. I was not only enormously grateful for all the gifts he gave me, but I also felt a great deal of affection for him. He turned out to be a kind generous man; he was never reactive, he was never anything. He was simply emotionally neutral. He was reliable, consistent and highly effective in his capacity to gift me. His generosity seemed boundless. He was, however, visibly relieved to have finally passed the lineage knowledge onto his student so that he could complete his life's work. There was nothing further for him to do in this life. He could relax and enjoy the rest of his time in his body, which is in fact exactly what he did.

I have all of the capacities he gifted me and I have continued to use them. Although don Manuel didn't necessarily have all the capacities he offered me, he did have the ability to transmit them. These were lineage capacities that he was the custodian of and could pass along to me. Don Manuel seemed to know that I had the ability to use these capacities, which I did in a series of healings that began at the start of the new millennium and continued over a thirteen-year period. I never saw don Manuel again. He died a few years later.

When don Manuel declared me his peer, he introduced me to the most refined energies of the higher realms—and gifted me the knowledge of, and fluency with, these energies. Don Manuel opened the door to the higher realms so that I now reside within the refined energy. I am a servant of these realms. They lack a unified consciousness and agency themselves, but they contain the wisdom I access when I listen to what wants to be known. It was from that realm that I was directed and allowed to heal don Mauricio a few years after I said goodbye to don Manuel. This is how it all happened.

A few of my students had implored me to introduce them to an indigenous shaman. I decided I would take three of them to visit the Tarahumara, a native group in Copper Canyon in northwestern Mexico. Copper Canyon is in a huge mountainous area—the Sierra Madre Occidental, which at the time was largely impenetrable. My student, Tim Collier, said he knew someone who knew someone who knew someone else who had a connection to the Tarahumara. So, three of us flew to El Paso, met up with Tim and proceeded to pick up our Hertz rent-a-car. Unfortunately, as soon as Hertz found out we planned to drive into Mexico, they refused to hand over the car. We ended up getting a pristine car from Avis—a huge Chevy sedan with low mileage. By the time we returned it, a couple of weeks later, it was completely trashed. Luckily, we bought the Avis insurance!

So we set off down the four-lane highway into the Chihuahuan desert. We spent the night in Chihuahua where I found a beautiful, old colonial church. It was a 16th century church, full of old icons and paintings and incense. The moment I entered, I felt the toxicity, the toxicity from thousands of people who, over the years, had walked in, dumped their negativity, felt better, and left. There hadn't been any priest at the church who could clear up the energy, so the negativity had gotten really thick. I stood in the church and I cleaned it up, neutralized all the negativity that had built up for God knows how long. And then I turned my attention to the icons, stimulating each one to awaken. Instead of taking from the icons, as worshippers had been doing for centuries, I gave to them. I gave them all a healing, I rejuvenated them so they could light up and begin functioning again, so that the church could awaken as well.

Outside the church, there were two fountains that no longer worked energetically so I took a little time waking them up, too. I knew how to do that because I had spent hours figuring that out when I was in Cusco. The Libertador Hotel, where I often stayed, had a beautiful ornate fountain from the 16th century, which also didn't work. I just kept playing with it until I got it to wake up, until it began to emanate an interesting enriching energy, which these fountains were meant to give off. They were more than sources of water; they were sources of spiritual refreshment.

The next morning, we headed off to Creel with an interpreter and a guide, figuring we'd either meet up with Tim's contact or something else would happen. No contact materialized. We hit the road again. Once we left Creel, the roads got worse and worse; the mountains more rugged and steep. After a couple of hours bouncing around, we ended up deep in the recesses of a remote valley, where we came across a group of people who obviously lived there. We got out of the car. Our interpreter immediately got into a conversation with a guy who spoke Tarahumara; the guy looked to be about 30 or 40, an indigenous man, dressed in native clothes. He then translated what was said into Spanish and our guide translated it into English for us.

I gathered from what was being said that there was an elderly man, a local spiritual healer, who might be available to meet me. Lots of questions went back and forth, as the men tried to figure out who the other three guys were who had accompanied me—and why they had come. So finally, I began to energetically establish a connection with the man our interpreter had been talking to. I just started to rely on whatever I could pass on telepathically to him and, fortunately, he got it. He understood that I wasn't a tourist, I wasn't afraid, and that I understood the protocols of these kinds of meetings. He offered to introduce me to his teacher. And I said, "Thank you, yes, I would like to meet him."

So he and I walked over to this little hut, which I hadn't noticed before. And out came this tiny, very old man, accompanied by an assistant; he was introduced to me as don Mauricio, and he addressed me as don Pablo. I treated him as a local spiritual leader of the highest stature—which is what he was, as the high priest in that area— and he in turn was most respectful of me. We connected telepathically right away and he invited me into his hut. Inside the hut were all kinds of herbs hanging from the ceiling, and a few mats on the floor to sit down on. His assistant would hand don Mauricio an herb, and through the interpreter, don Mauricio would explain its significance. It was then that it dawned on me that he was blind. At one point, he paused to explain that his wife was away and apologized that I would be unable to meet her.

After we left the hut and went back outside, don Mauricio indicated that he would like to show me his church. So, we all squeezed into a Jeep—including my students—and drove into another canyon where we stopped at a tiny Roman Catholic church, which looked to me as though it could fall over if the wind picked up. Behind the altar, in a room closed off by a door, there was a closet, out of which don Mauricio's assistant took some flags and long poles with Christian crosses made of silver mounted on them. These objects were of tremendous importance to don Mauricio and I indicated how much I admired and appreciated them. I was truly quite moved by his willingness to show me these sacred objects because, after all, we had just met. Then, don Mauricio indicated it was time to go to another remote spot—even deeper into nowhere.

After awhile, we came to another valley where we stopped at a small cattle ranch, the property of Mestizo man, whom everyone in the four-wheeler knew. He welcomed all of us. After the introductions don Mauricio announced that he had been waiting a long time for me and that he was ready for me to heal his blindness. I asked the interpreter to translate what don Mauricio just said twice, because I wasn't so sure I got it the first time. By now, there were two dozen native people standing around, too, all of them looking at me. It was hot. We were in the sun in the middle of the field; don Mauricio walked over to an open area adjacent to the ranch house, and stood there waiting.

I became aware of my vulnerability. I hadn't a clue where I was. Nor did I know how to leave, if I had to. So if I couldn't help him I didn't know what might happen next. I reminded myself that I had been giving healings since I was young; I had responded to scores of requests for healings in the Andes as well. It wasn't as though I had to do something I hadn't done my whole life. I also was acutely aware that I hadn't a clue how to heal this

PART TWO: MY JOURNEY TO PERU

guy. No one had ever asked me to restore their eyesight before. And the sun was really bothering me—I had taken my hat off earlier to show my respect to don Mauricio. I was hot and thirsty and hungry.

I asked for a chair, sat him down in the bright afternoon sun and then stood over him waiting for what wanted to be known. I lost all conscious awareness for a while and, when I came to, I was still standing over him. I watched as he opened his eyes. He turned around to face me and I saw a big smile on his face. It was only then that I began to know the extent of the gifting I had received from Don Manuel. Don Mauricio stood up, began walking around, moving his head from side to side. Still smiling from ear to ear, he started talking in an animated way in Tarahumara. All the people standing around just mobbed him, without touching him, of course—nobody would touch such a venerable figure—and started talking all at once. They couldn't believe what had just happened! They were stunned. Mauricio could see! He could see very clearly. He was so happy that he just couldn't stop smiling, couldn't stop talking. And neither could anyone else.

Finally he quieted down and then everyone followed suit. And after a while I suggested that we all get out of the sun. So we sat on the porch of the ranch house in the shade and I asked if he'd be willing to explain to my students how he performed his healings. He generously agreed and told them he was a traditional herbal healer and a breath healer, a gift he had been given by another traditional healer. He literally exhales a healing energy onto the individual he's working with.

We stayed another hour or so before saying our goodbyes and heading back to the motel in Creel. Apparently, word spread quickly that don Mauricio had been healed by an Andean priest, and by the time we woke up the next morning, a fairly large group of people had gathered outside my room, hoping to be healed. I responded the best I could, but I don't really remember much about the specifics. I do remember that I was still communicating telepathically with don Mauricio, trying to ascertain whether I'd have to go back again for a second healing or whether what I had done had been sufficient. We came to the conclusion that the one healing had worked and that I was free to go.

The next couple days were devoted to exploring Copper Canyon. The Canyon is stunningly beautiful, much like Chaco Canyon, with a wonderful energetic quality. As we were leaving the Sierra, I asked that we stop the car for a moment. I wanted to get out and connect once again with don Mauricio. I stood next to a stream and found his energy. I said goodbye to him telepathically and, in that moment, he reciprocated. In that moment, he gave me a transmission, the gift of breath healing. So I am now, thanks to don Mauricio, capable of healing with the breath.

PART TWO: MY JOURNEY TO PERU

Looking back on my time in the Andes, I realized that the moment don Manuel smashed me on the back, I lost my ability to say anything, to ask him questions. I wasn't even capable of saying, "Well what are you going to teach me?" or "why do you want to teach me?" I was never able to question why I would want to do this or why I should care about any of this or who this guy was. I was only able to say, "Yes."

During our time together I always said, "Yes." Dozens of times he invited me to risk my life and I said, "Yes." I was willing to do that because I trusted that he would never abuse our relationship. And he never did. My entire experience with him—face-to-face and in my dreams—was a "yes," and my life continues to be "Yes." There's never been any doubt; no "what or why?" Only yes. And it is still "yes."

Over the years, I've learned to be better at listening for 'what wants to be known' so I know what I'm saying "yes" to, but whatever it is that wants to be known, I respond to it with a "yes." No matter how unpleasant or outrageous it's been, I say "yes."

Lord Pakal
and the
Nine Lords of Time

A few months before my first trip to Cusco, I was invited by a small group of professional psychics to travel to Palenque, a vast archaeological zone in the jungles of Chiapas, a low lying area in southern Mexico bordering on Guatemala. It was 1990, I was almost 50 years old and I had never been out of the United States. From the photographs I saw, Palenque looked like a big amusement park; it somehow reminded me of the photos I had seen of the pyramids in Egypt. All of which is to say I knew nothing about Palenque. I just happened to be dating one of the psychics in the group so I jumped at the chance to join in the fun.

We arrived at Palenque, touching down in the smallest airport I had ever seen. I was surprised by how remote the area was back then. Spiritual tourism wasn't yet a thing, so we pretty much had the place to ourselves. Granted, the accommodations were limited and so were the food choices, but the weather was mild with no rain in the forecast.

Ever since I was a child I played around in the spirit world, a realm in which I lived, much like my grandmother Gussie. I loved it. I learned to heal using the powers from the spirit realm and even to protect myself from attacking spirits. But as a kid, and even a teenager, I loved to amuse myself by attacking other spirits.

So, on my first afternoon at Palenque, I thought I would have some really good fun. At the first temple we visited, I stood at the edge of the pavilion, the approach to the temple itself and, on a whim, began to throw a little energy at the heart of it, taunting it, teasing and provoking it. I didn't really mean anything by my actions; I was just being playfully disrespectful. I continued hurling energy at it until I got bored. And suddenly the temple had had enough. A huge fireball came rolling out of it, flattening me onto the stone walkway and knocking me unconscious. After a while, I came to and was able to stand up, thanks to the women in my group, but I was still pretty shaken. That was no fun at all. Nevertheless I had no plans to give up quite yet. I was determined to enjoy myself.

At another one of the temples, I noticed a strong upward movement of energy, swirling clockwise within the inner sanctum of the temple. I jumped right into it and it spit me right back out and I landed on all fours. This time I learned my lesson. Whatever was here was potent. This was no playground, this was no Coney Island. Something was definitely going on.

The rest of the trip was pretty uneventful. I returned home and a few months later set off to Peru in hopes of expanding my capacity for healing others. Nevertheless, something called me back to Palenque and a year or so later, I heeded the call. This time I was alone and curious and decidedly more polite, reverent, and careful. Maybe Palenque had something to teach me, as well, something that would help me become a more competent healer.

One of my first stops was at the Temple of Inscriptions, a rather large pyramid featured prominently in the excavated area of Palenque. By then I had done my homework. I knew the temple was the burial site of the most important king of Palenque, Lord Pakal, who died in the latter part of the seventh century. Lord Pakal supervised the building of the temple during the first ten years of its construction and then, shortly after Pakal's death, his son took over and completed it.

Lord Pakal was an extraordinary esoteric master, without peer in the Mayan world. The sarcophagus lid, or covering, on his tomb is probably the best known single piece of art from Mesoamerica. It continues to attract academic speculation, popular speculation and the admiration all sorts of people who are attracted to the aesthetic of

PART TWO: MY JOURNEY TO PERU

Palenque. The lid shows Pakal in a rather odd position. He's not stretched out lying in state; rather he's crouched down, surrounded by all kinds of decoration, lineage information and important dates about him. The walls of his crypt are decorated with representations of the nine spirits who are his protectors, his bodyguards.

I walked up the stone staircase, which was a difficult climb because its dimensions were odd—the risers were too high and the steps themselves too narrow. At the top I noticed another set of stairs, which led into the bowels of the temple. Walking down those stairs made me quite uneasy. There was no light to guide my way; no handrail to hold on to. The stone was slippery and I was convinced that one misstep would result in an endless slide to god knows where. With a long line of tourists in front and in back of me, any misstep by anyone would literal crush us all. I managed to get down to the bottom in what felt like a very deep sub-basement; it was poorly lit and crowded with tourists—from the States, Europe, and Japan mostly. I could barely breathe. I saw no Mexicans, certainly no Mayans. A guard stood at the bottom of the stairs ushering people in and moving them along. He didn't want anyone to linger. People came down the steps and stared into the burial chamber that was blocked off by a locked metal gate until the guard told them to leave.

So anyway, I had my moment in front of the

sarcophagus and I turned and walked back up the stairs, happy to greet the daylight and relieved to get some air. I had felt claustrophobic and the combination of a closed, dank atmosphere and the lack of fresh air was beginning to make me panic. Weirdly, the moment I surfaced I knew something had transpired, something I wasn't able to articulate. All I knew, because I had been raised in the realm of the spirits, was that I had somehow connected with a spirit—and that spirit may have been Pakal's.

I made a dozen or more trips to visit Lord Pakal in the Temple of Inscriptions. I was fascinated by Palenque and quite interested in the esoteric qualities of the Maya. On one particular journey in the mid-90s, an American celebrity couple hired me to guide them on a trip through a half dozen Mayan archaeological zones, some of which I had never been to before. Our first stop was Palenque. By that time, the Temple of Inscriptions was closed to the public because the interior of the temple had weakened as a result of all the foot traffic. Of course, this celebrity couple could visit Pakal's tomb by virtue of their status, which meant that I could, too. So the three of us walked down the stairs. No one else was there, not even a guard, and no lights to guide our way. I turned on my flashlight. The stairs felt more slippery than ever; the air more dank and lifeless. The three of us paused at the burial chamber. But almost immediately, the couple I was with insisted on leaving. I remained there, alone in the complete silence, for what seemed like a long time. I flipped off the flashlight and simply stood there. Much like don Manuel did, the spirit of Pakal welcomed me and began offering me gifts, more gifts and more gifts. He presented himself to me as a skilled master of the stars, traveling through the celestial sphere on an endless journey of celebration. At the time I had no cognitive sense of what I was being given, but I was quite certain that I was being filled up. I never asked him why I was being given these transmissions. I never asked what I was supposed to do with them. I simply remained as open as I could, in this airless, closed-in space. I felt so fortunate to have had the experiences I had with my first teacher, Gussie, who invited me into her world when I was only three years old. She taught me how to become fluent within the esoteric world of a master teacher. Although I didn't understand what it was that Pakal was teaching me, I did know how to receive it. I knew that I was filled up each time I visited him.

So, there I was in front of the burial chamber of a king who had died more than a thousand years ago, receiving what he had to offer as though he were my teacher and very much alive. Truthfully, my experience was not so unusual. It's actually traditional for people to visit tombs or other sacred places and receive teachings, revelations, insights, and even profound transformations they have no words to describe. Those who visit Rumi's tomb at Kona or the tomb of St. James in Santiago de Compostela or journey to Mecca, to the Sacred Stone—the examples are endless—often come away forever changed. And, so it was for me. I come from a tradition where it's not at all unusual to learn from a departed master at gravesites, receive gifts, revelations and teachings.

Finally at some point it was time to say goodbye. I promised to return—I knew there would be more for me—and then I walked back up the stairs. I felt like I had overeaten, or had drunk too much beer; it was a heavy unpleasant feeling. By the time I got to the top of the interior staircase and walked out into the daylight, the early afternoon of bright sunlight had become a late afternoon of uncharacteristically darkened skies. As I descended the outer stairs, I realized that we were in for a major, out-of-season storm. Fifteen minutes later, on the veranda of my casita, just a short distance from the archaeological zone, I sat and watched as a ferocious tropical storm approached, bringing with it torrential rains and high winds. A storm so unexpected that no one was prepared for it. It went on all evening and into the night.

By dawn it was over and the skies were clear. In the aftermath, trees were flattened, roads closed and areas flooded. I knew all this because we left Palenque that morning, on the private plane we had arrived on, and I could see the destruction below. I suddenly understood: Pakal had sent

PART TWO: MY JOURNEY TO PERU

the storm as a way to mark the encounter I had had with him. It was his way of acknowledging a new student.

One night, a couple of weeks later, I was back home in Sausalito, sound asleep, when I suddenly became aware that I had visitors: nine warrior spirits who Lord Pakal sent to protect me from any and all attacks within the spirit realm. These spirits have many names because the translations from the Mayan glyphs aren't always consistent. Sometimes called The Nine Lords of Time, Nine Lords of Death, or even Nine Lords of the Night, these guardians show up on the walls of Pakal's tomb. These spirits stayed with me, traveled with me, kept very close to me for the next decade or so, protecting me whenever I stepped into a situation that was hostile or negative and I was in danger of attack. Pakal's warrior spirits, his bodyguards, had become my bodyguards and they were as potent as anything one could encounter in the spirit realm. They were quick and efficient. Nothing could penetrate them. I felt safe and protected, knowing that these warrior spirits could take care of any situation handily.

I knew that he had gifted me with protection against attack. I knew that he was continually available to me if I needed to consult with him. I knew that he was very supportive of what I was about to do, although I didn't know what I was about to do. I was simply putting one foot in front of the next, moving into an unknown, one step at a time. As I moved into this unknown there was continual revelation, occasional confusion and definitely some missteps. This unknown began for me right at the turn of the millennium and it went on for over a decade. During that time Pakal's support never faltered and was always crucial.

Still, the night those Nine Lords of Time appeared at my bedside, I had no idea what they'd be protecting me from or what Lord Pakal had in mind when he sent them to me. As it turned out, the gifts he gave me saved my life more than once. But, as I would discover, they came with some serious obligations—to him and to don Manuel. And I had to fulfill those obligations before the spirits could return home and take up residence once again at the Temple of Inscriptions.

Lord Pakal gifted me in a way that's hard to describe. Clearly, by lending me the protection of his Nine Lords, he would never allow any harm to come to me when I was being of service. That gift was especially important because I definitely experienced times when I was not at my best—I was ill or exhausted, upset or confused—and I knew I would be safe.

Like I said, Lord Pakal was the Supreme Master of celestial navigation. Those within his lineage—male and female—were masters of celestial spheres. They moved through star fields as cosmic athletes. He gifted me with that capacity also, although it's not something I use because my work is focused on service. Lord Pakal and his lineage possessed extraordinary, esoteric charisma; they were masters of subtle energy emanation, a capacity he also gifted to me. I've used that capacity to command a wide range of subtle energies, and even to create subtle energies.

PART THREE

FULFILLING MY OBLIGATIONS

Receiving Through Imitation

I have an important skill set that I've maintained ever since I was a very young child—a skill that every child has, in fact—the ability to imitate others. Imitation is how I learned from my teachers; it is how I learned to listen to what wants to be known. I could witness them, not with my eyes but with my full capacity. I could witness them by being fully open to them, by not being defensive or suspicious. I always made myself available to them and allowed myself to absorb whatever I was witnessing.

The way I was taught was to be invited in, so that I could become absorbed within the being of the teacher, receive the transmissions, and hold them—and obtain the protection of the teacher at the same time. I absorbed everything and retained everything because I never had any doubts. I was 100 percent open to my teachers and whatever I witnessed, I accepted. And I accepted ownership of it. I was literally the mirror of my teacher moment-to-moment and I allowed myself to be as clear a mirror as I could be.

Sitting at the table next to Gussie I would watch everything she did; I would feel into the silence and take in whatever she offered. She never spoke and so I was obligated to listen intently, open myself up so that I could assimilate the gifts she was offering me; to watch and learn what I needed to learn in order to serve others.

It was the same with all of my teachers.

Just like with Gussie, most of my time with don Manuel was spent in silence, watching and waiting, imitating and receiving. And yet, I wasn't able to receive all that he wanted to "gift" me until I could release my fears—of heights, of dying—and anything else that stood in my way of being open and receptive. Unlike with Gussie, I couldn't always tell what don Manuel was giving me; all I knew was that, toward the end of each long night, I felt a fullness—or even an overload—within. In fact, I didn't always understand what capacities any of my teachers were giving me—not right away—nor how they intended me to use them. But I was always happy to have them at my disposal.

I use the power of imitation out in the world, as well. A few years before I met don Manuel, I used to visit the old growth Redwoods in Northern California and had started a practice of sitting daily in their hollowed out trunks. I would hike and walk the beach and often nap outdoors. And then, in 1987, on one of my outings, I met Dan Harvey, an extraordinary athlete, aspirant Zen monk and student of an indigenous priest. Dan taught me how to walk more easily and effortlessly. His verbal instruction was useful, of course, but mostly, I learned by walking next to him. I would imitate his gait and breathing pattern at first and, then, his general body awareness. After we'd been walking together, Dan introduced me to indoor rock-wall climbing and showed me strength and endurance exercises, all the while climbing and exercising right along with me. My imitation of Dan was so thorough that I transformed into him. Not that I became a tall, blond, blue-eyed former male model but, in a deeper sense, I did become Dan Harvey.

Tragically, Dan died in a motorcycle accident while I was studying with don Manuel.

One early morning, a year or so after Dan's death, I was sitting on a gym floor, stretching, when I began to have a strong sense of Dan stretching next to me. In that moment, Dan gifted me with his strong sense of physicality, of being continuously aware of this moment as a moment to be experienced within my physical body.

Imitation is how you open yourself up to receive the gifts your teacher offers you. It's how you learn. But in order to use the gifts, you need a teacher's permission. Again, Gussie taught me many things when I was a child, including the warrior skills I needed so I could defend myself and function both in the Bronx and within the spirit realm. She also gifted me with the capacities of our family lineage. However, I didn't have permission to use those capacities until Gussie's daughter Harriet officially acknowledged me as lineage head, almost twenty years after Gussie's death. Don Manuel gave me permission when he declared that the teachings were over and that I was now a high Andean priest and his peer. When Lord Pakal lent me his nine lords for protection, he gave me permission to use them in any way that I needed for my protection.

With both Gussie and don Manuel, I was more than just their student; I was their designated heir. I inherited everything and I had to be trained to carry it all, embody it all, and contain it all. If I couldn't use it all—and no one really presumed that I would—I could pass it on. Neither Gussie nor Manuel had the physical health to use everything they inherited; but they did have the capacity to pass it on. My relationship with Lord Pakal was different. I was never his heir; I was just a student who was taught specific capacities and given permission to use them—and was offered protection as I fulfilled my obligations to him and to don Manuel.

I remember how don Manuel used to sit on a rock in the afternoon and play his flute for his llamas. As I watched him, I realized he was doing much more than soothing his herd. He was caring for the land, healing the negativity of the Q'eros region after it had been weakened by human action—and returning the land to a healthy, clean, clear, high vibrational state. By doing so, he was fulfilling a traditional obligation of the land steward to maintain the consciousness of the natural and human worlds of his region.

Don Manuel regularly gave prayer offerings to the sacred mountains and a sacred lake in the region and they, in turn, continuously blessed the Q'eros region and its people. As high priest, it was his obligation to maintain this sacred reciprocity. As he worked, I merged into him energetically. So watching him was like watching him from the inside or, to put it differently, experiencing him as he fulfilled his obligations as the steward of Q'eros.

Taking him into my body allowed me, over time, to take on that function myself and, in the early 90s, I became the steward of the little town of Sausalito where I lived. I took on the challenge of healing all the negativity deposited on its waterfront, beginning in World War II. Back then, Sausalito's waterfront was a vast factory in which ninety-three cargo vessels and tankers—so-called "Liberty ships"—were built and launched onto Richardson Bay, a shallow, ecologically rich arm of the larger San Francisco Bay. The negativity stemmed from the 24/7 construction and the pollution it caused as well as from the prostitution, gambling, drugs and violence that had been rampant since the late 1800s. By the time I moved to town, the coast guard had stopped the drug smuggling; the police shut down the gambling and prostitution rings, and the violence had abated. But the residue of all that remained.

It took me about six years to transform Sausalito. I worked on it daily, sometimes twice a day. As I did, I came up against the problem of ghosts, souls who had been wandering the land after the traumatic death of the individual within whom these souls lived. These souls or ghosts would wander in confusion and they would wander indefinitely. I had been encountering ghostly souls ever since I was a teenager when I tried to heal the battlefields in the States. Much later, when I was a student of Juan Nuñez del Prado, I discovered I could gently coax souls into going home. That's exactly what I did in Sausalito.

Over the years I have created a high vibrational quality within the city and it has become an energetically pleasant place to live. I've also become a steward of one of the beaches in West Marin—Limantour Beach—and more recently Tomales Bay, just adjacent to Limantour. Being a steward, being responsible for a land area, is time consuming and physically demanding.

My active and thorough imitation of each of my spiritual teachers and my openness to receiving their gifts transformed me into each of them. I have become them although there is no outward sign. And I have their permission to be each of them and to actively use the gifts they each bestowed. I continue the traditions of my teachers by giving gifts of healing and gifts of blessing.

A New Beginning— But of What?

On a full moon not long after my fear died, I stood outside don Manuel's house and listened as he explained the significance of that moon. Its intense brightness stood out against an unusually cloudless, fogless sky. Don Manuel declared that this moon signaled the start of a new time. He didn't specify what was new, but kept emphasizing a new beginning and a new time. Nothing else seemed particularly important in this short speech other than the implication that don Manuel's lineage had a function to perform in the 'new time.'

I had no idea what he was talking about. I had certainly heard all kinds of prophecies since I had been in the Andes—about the return of the Inca, the return of the Christ and a 'harmonic convergence.' At first I thought that don Manuel's 'new time' prediction referred to something external, like a "regime change" or a promise of material prosperity for everyone. I couldn't figure out why he was telling me all that (through an interpreter, of course) or what it had to do with me. All I knew was that he meant for me to assist in that "new beginning." In fact, as it turned out, I was obligated to devote my life to making it happen.

My obligations to this prophecy put me off at first. Don Manuel had involved me, had in fact trained me to undertake the lineage obligations he himself could not or would not undertake. Over time, I discovered that I was trained to take don Manuel's lineage wisdom to the West and to take on the responsibility for 'birthing' this prophecy.

It took several years before I realized that he was announcing a transformation within the higher or upper realms of the Sacred, a transformation whose impact on the material realm might not be readily obvious.

Relinquishing My Lineages

The first few years after I said my final goodbyes to don Manuel were difficult ones for me. My personal and professional life unraveled as I struggled to locate myself in the day to day of the States. Q'eros was now my spiritual home and, in important ways, I was more comfortable with its people than with 'Europeans.' I considered moving to Cusco but finally decided against it. Don Manuel had wanted me to remain in the 'European' world and, besides, there was apparently considerable suspicion of me by Peruvian and American security services. So I took daily car rides from my Sausalito apartment to the old growth Redwood groves and beaches of California's north coast for inspiration, camped at Chaco Canyon for reassurance, and presented myself at Lord Pakal's for sanctuary. I struggled, seemingly caught between the traditional and the post-modern.

PART THREE: FULFILLING MY OBLIGATIONS

During that time, a group of twenty or so spiritual seekers used to gather in the large living room of my rented house in Sausalito. They were witnesses to a ceremonial event modelled on my evenings with don Manuel. Each evening centered on my creating and then burning one of the many despacho I had learned. The foundation of a despacho is an arrangement of coca leaves on top of which is piled candies, seeds, nuts, a llama fetus, and other things, all of which I had brought back in my luggage from the Andes. Offering a despacho is another example of the use of ordinary items for ritual magic.

After a lifetime of practicing ritual magic, what wanted to be known was surprising and unprecedented for me: Ritual magic had become a distraction from my obligations. Without permission I stopped all traditional ritual practices and gifted my mesa, candlesticks and drinking glass to San Francisco Bay at Point Bonita. I was now free, at age fifty five to explore daily spiritual practice outside the context of ritual magic.

All the while I remained within the realm of the spirits. The material realm, the everyday, was secondary. Like Gussie and don Manuel, I had lived my life within the spirit realm. This was my known, familiar venue. Needless to say, I was not very practical when it came to managing income, career, retirement and all that sort of thing. The spirit realm is a soulless, timeless, and dimensionless arena of powerful, coherent energies, which are either menacing or indifferent. These energies or entities are different from ghosts, which are disembodied souls, temporarily misplaced. The spirit realm has no internal dynamics other than its qualities of conflict and randomness; it is a world without beginning, end, or purpose. A conflict is expressed as a forceful exchange of energies that doesn't lead to bloodshed, death or destruction—it merely generates more conflict. Feelings and emotions are unknown. This is a timeless realm free of values and purpose. Change is constant and yet, oddly, nothing changes. Gussie, who of course also lived in the spirit world, showed me how to protect myself from menacing spirits and the dangerous individuals who manipulated them. At a very young age, I became a 'warrior' in the spirit realm.

For don Manuel, the spirit realm was home to the spirits of mountains, lakes, rivers, and other parts of the natural world; the realm in which he expressed his devotion and service. He was trained as a priest, rather than a warrior, and as such, he prayed to the mountain spirits of the Q'eros region and taught me to do the same. Jesus and Mother Mary, especially Mother Mary, were two of the most important spirits. Don Manuel gifted me with an advanced esoteric teaching about the spirit realm. His gift gave me the capacity to step out of the spirit realm and yet be able to communicate with this realm and mobilize its energy, which is what I would need when I began the

PART THREE: FULFILLING MY OBLIGATIONS

transformative healings he had tasked me with, during the 'new time' that began in 2000.

I stayed in the spirit realm after don Manuel "graduated," me, because I was obligated to defend his lineage, as well as my family's, against any spirit challengers that showed up. I was also required to energetically "feed" the lineages of all three—Gussie, don Manuel, Lord Pakal—as an expression of reciprocity. In return, I continued to receive transmissions and 'support.'

When I was younger, these spirit world conflicts were amusing and challenging distractions, my version of playing tennis or soccer or watching TV. But by the mid- to late-90s, these challenges took on a more intense, warlike quality because my status in the spirit realm had changed. I was no longer playing. Rather, now I was in serious combat with multiple challengers intent on humiliating my lineages. At that time I was also teaching a dozen novices the basics of spirit world navigation and I was having a difficult time protecting them from attacking spirits. I was gaining a new insight trying to teach this group of novices: Admission to the spirit realm is only possible at birth. The art of spirit world navigation cannot be taught to adults not born into this realm.

Slowly and painfully, I began to consider living outside the spirit realm. Not only had combat intensified, but I was also getting more demands for 'juice' from my lineages—which took its toll. I was tired. The more distracted I became by the conflicts and demands, the harder it became to settle into a life in the West. I knew no one to discuss all this with and my confusion became disorientation. My mental health was threatened. Paradoxically, I finally concluded that I had to break my lineage ties and renounce the spirit realm so that I could fulfill my obligations to don Manuel and Lord Pakal. I was beginning to sense that I would be obligated to navigate the higher realms, perhaps even the highest spiritual realms to help birth the planetary renewal foreseen by don Manuel. Continuing to live with the spirits would block me from my obligations.

I decided to cleanse myself. I would expel Gussie and don Manuel from inside of me and break all energetic connections with all the spirits of these lineages. So I began to listen to what wanted to be known and I rapidly came to 'know' how to proceed. Looking back at it now with the hindsight of more than two decades, it looks like an angry mob attacking a victim and the victim refusing to remain a victim. I fought back. It morphed into a street brawl reminiscent of high school gang fights of my teen years in New York. I kept fighting and losing. There were too many of them. We were all throwing balls of energy at each other in a timeless, dimensionless brawl. In clock time, this brawl went on for a month or more and finally they just let me go because the alternative was to remain in perpetual conflict, which would have destroyed my physical health.

PART THREE: FULFILLING MY OBLIGATIONS

I was now my own person for the first time in my life and it was nothing short of a rebirth for me. I was meeting myself as new and at first, I did not like it. I was alone. No Gussie or don Manuel as constant, intimate companions. It was then that I discovered that the natural world, more specifically old growth Redwoods and remote California beaches, were a doorway directly into the higher spiritual realms. And these were the realms I would now navigate as I fulfilled my obligations to don Manuel.

Dissolving the Occult Triangle

Late one night, about two or three years after don Manuel and I parted company I woke up out of a vivid dream, a dream in which don Manuel had gifted me with a new healing capacity. Over the next few years, he continued to appear in my dreams and offer me capacities; there were about a dozen of these gifts in total. Some of them were healing capacities, others were capacities I didn't understand and had no idea how to use. I came to realize that these gifts, which had initially been embedded in me while we were asleep together in Chua Chua, had lain dormant and were awakening in me in a certain sequence and timing that were mysterious to me. Around the same time, I began to have dreams that spoke to me about visiting Europe.

I had never been to Europe, and I had no interest in going. Europe was the old world, I was interested in the new world. And yet these dreams persisted. The message in each of them was clear: I must go to Europe because there was service I was required to do and it could only be done in Europe. And, it was time.

Finally, in November of 1999, I decided I needed to go. I called my friend, Philippe, who was living in Paris at the time, and asked him if he'd be willing to drive me around France. I told him that I was looking for something but I wasn't sure yet what it was. He agreed to meet me in two weeks.

On a pleasantly warm afternoon, days before I left California, I headed out to Point Reyes National Park and turned onto Pierce Point Road, where a herd of tule elk often grazes. Tule elk, at least the males, get very large and can be quite aggressive, especially during mating season. So I'm always cautious and respectful. But it was late December, so I wasn't worried; they are usually quite docile and a little standoffish.

I pulled my car over to the side of the road and got out to say hello to a small group of elk gathered nearby—one bull and three or four cows. I was interested in meeting whomever was interested in meeting me. I stood there for a moment, said hello, and waited to see if anyone would respond. The elk were, I don't know, maybe a hundred yards, maybe 75 yards from me. Reasonably close. I slowly walked towards them until I got close enough to see them clearly but within a distance I sensed was their comfort zone. Finally, after maybe a half hour of this sort of thing, the big guy, the bull, looked at me. I looked at him and we just said hello and hello and hello. After a while the hello deepened to, "I would like to meet you at the level of your strength." And the big guy agreed. "Okay, I'm receptive to meeting you as I am. I'm perfectly comfortable if you'd like to taste my strength and since you're not predatory, you can have a gift of my strength."

So there was an offer. I welcomed that offer because it was what I wanted. I wanted that strength, it's the quality I have seen, the quality I have witnessed in tule elk, especially the males. They have a certain courage and steadfastness that I have long admired and that I knew I would need during my trip. I was going off to Europe in search of a church, a 12th or 13th century church somewhere in France, and I had to be prepared for what might happen when I found it. I had to be courageous. I had to be resolute. Never having been in a medieval church, never having been in France, having no sense of what spirits I might encounter or what the energetics might be, I didn't know what I was opening myself to. So I wanted to be as strong and unwavering as I could be. Very rapidly I was filled up with this very strong, potent, almost fierce courage and steadfastness, resoluteness. I was grateful to this elk for its generosity. After a while I thanked him and reciprocated by offering him a healing gift. And then I got back in my car and went home.

PART THREE: FULFILLING MY OBLIGATIONS

There were other moments when I stopped to visit the elk. Moments when I sensed that I would need an extra measure of courage and resoluteness in order to meet what was about to confront me. Each time I revisited the elk at Point Reyes, I was gifted with a wonderful strength—a courage that continued to serve me on these journeys—that just seemed endless.

Hours before the new millennium, I flew to Paris and Philippe picked me up from the airport in a very old car. Philippe was a post-modern sadhu, a French wild man and spiritual adventurer, willing to drive all over France, during what the media dubbed "the storm of the century," which brought terrible rains and high winds, flooding and mass destruction. And that's exactly what we did. Until, in Normandy, we slid off the road into a ditch and our journey came to an end. We were literally stuck in Normandy, just outside of a little village, cold, wet, and hungry. Some lovely people took us in and put us up for the night. I asked the man if there was a church in the village and he said yes, it was a 12th-century church. He had the keys to it and was happy to take me there and happy to let me stay as long as I wanted. I found myself both hesitant to enter—worried about what might await me—and filled with the courage and resoluteness of this wonderful tule elk from Point Reyes.

The back of the church had what looked like barn doors. It was as if a rider could ride his horse up to the back of the church, the doors would open, and they would both enter the church, long enough for the rider to dismount; someone else would lead the horse away. Those doors seemed like a convenience to the local lord, whose church it was.

The church was really very cold; the temperature inside even colder than the temperature outside. Everything was stone, and kneeling in front of the altar was quite distressing. The cold came in through my knees from the stone. As I knelt at the altar, I suddenly lost any awareness of my surroundings; I fainted and fell onto the stone.

Lying there, I had an intense, vivid dream. I was back in 12th-century Normandy in the church, when the back doors opened up and the lord of the village appeared. He was quite charismatic and perhaps somewhat tyrannical. He was ritually dressed in black and wore a sword. He stood there, surveying the church, which was full of his serfs. In the dream, I was the priest, also all dressed in black, and he and I were in some kind of conflict with each other. The conflict was resolved when I acquiesced to him, to his presence, his command, his authority. It was that acquiescence that had long remained a limitation within my capacity. It was that limitation, that acquiescence to established authority that I had to shed.

The dream continued. The church was empty and I was kneeling in front of the altar. As I prayed, I became cleansed of that incapacity. What made the difference, what enabled me to shed that acquiescence, that limitation within my consciousness, within my awareness, was the energetic gift from the elk at Point Reyes. From then on—in the following weeks and months and years that I continued traveling in Europe and Latin America to respond to the obligations of my teachers—I was no longer hindered by this incapacity.

Philippe and I hung around Normandy for a few more days before I headed back to San Francisco. I felt lighter and unburdened. A month or so later, I was back, and I returned every couple of months, spending two weeks in France with each visit. I gave teachings and public talks; I offered healings and visited sacred places. But I couldn't help wondering why I was in Europe. What was I supposed to be doing there?

After I'd been visiting France off and on for about a year, I met a woman from Paris who offered to show me around. I told her I'd had a recurring dream about meeting a member of my family lineage who was European; in the dream I saw him and I knew him immediately. I even saw the neighborhood he lived in. This woman walked with me all through this neighborhood, but we never found him. After a while, I came to know, through a dream, that he had died and I would never have the chance to meet him. He had been killed, murdered in the early '40s. I was grief stricken. I had long hoped I could find some connection within Europe that would allow me to meet other members of my family lineage—or members of other lineages that were associated with or similar to it. I continued to wonder what I was doing in Europe. One reason soon became clear: a few months later, the woman who had been showing me around Paris became my wife, and we have been happily together ever since.

During another one of my visits to France, I stayed near the Cathedral of Chartres for a week. At night, I walked its labyrinth and sat in its massive sanctuary after visiting hours. I met a mystic who sang medieval hymns with an exquisite voice to the interior structure of the sanctuary.

After Chartres, I prayed at the uncorrupted body of Saint Catherine Labouré that lies in repose in Paris, and visited with the 'heart' of Richard the Lionheart in the Cathédrale Notre-Dame de Rouen. I went on to visit other tombs, sacred relics, cemeteries, churches, synagogues, mosques, and healing places throughout Europe, where I was given strong teachings, guidance and inspiration and, in return, I offered teachings to the curious and healings to the needy. Visiting a relic, a tomb, or a sacred cave is an encounter with the mystery contained within that place. I was taught to approach with patience and openness, have purpose to my visit rather than curiosity, and to offer reverent prayer. My journey had permission from my teachers who had taught me the necessary skills to access these sacred places.

One afternoon, a woman I knew, who was Ital-

PART THREE: FULFILLING MY OBLIGATIONS

ian and had an inherited aristocratic title, asked me what I knew about the Black Occult Triangle, and I said, "Nothing. Never heard of it." In fact, when I researched it, I couldn't find anything written; no one, it seemed, had ever heard of it. She described it as information from the Vatican, from the Secretariat and offered to introduce me if I wanted the details. I declined. She then proceeded to tell me what she knew about it. Apparently, this powerful occult phenomenon was located in three cities—Lyon in France, Prague in the Czech Republic, and Turin in northern Italy. It was a powerful force, a force that had vied for influence and control amid all the conflicts in Western, Central, and Eastern Europe.

I sat and listened to what wanted to be known. Before long, it became clear to me that I was to disrupt this triangle. And, in order to do that, I would have to visit these locations and take whatever action I needed to take.

Problem was, I had no clue how to disrupt a dark occult force. I started researching Léon and discovered that in the 19th century a particular neighborhood had been a favorite of occultists; in the center of that neighborhood was a medieval Roman Catholic Church. I could see from the photos I found that this church was, in fact, the location of one of the points of the Dark Occult Triangle and that I would need to visit this church to engage this occult force field. That is precisely what I did.

WHAT WANTS TO BE KNOWN

When I returned to France a few weeks later, along with thirteen Americans, we went directly to Léon. These Americans were there to serve as my witnesses, I needed witnesses to provide a social context for what I was about to do. I couldn't do it in secret or in isolation. I walked into the church with the Americans trailing behind me. Unfortunately they weren't the most reliable witnesses because they were frightened, convinced that the occult force field, or whatever was defending it, would attack them. I realized that their fear and anxiety could easily be a distraction so I distanced myself from them, both physically and energetically, and proceeded to take a seat close to the main altar. I wasn't frightened because I knew that, no matter what went down, I had the protection of Lord Pakal's nine lords of time.

The force field was, indeed, located at the main altar. And oddly enough, nothing appeared to be defending it. In fact, it appeared to be an artifact from earlier in the 20th century or maybe even in the 19th century. The force field was in a very weakened state, so I had no trouble dissolving it. I offered it a loving kindness energy and as my offering entered it, the field quickly dissolved. I couldn't have been in the church for more than an hour when I bowed and took my leave. We walked around this old neighborhood, which was hundreds of years old, and we discovered many buildings decorated with Zodiac signs and other such occult symbols. However, the neighborhood had been updated and was now a fashionable location for dining and strolling about. My thirteen witnesses and I enjoyed a pleasant afternoon in the historic district, which was full of tourists, all having a good time. We sat in a restaurant and enjoyed the meal and then went on our way. One side of the dark occult triangle no longer existed.

Next up was the St. Vitus cathedral in Prague, the fulcrum of the triangle. We arrived there a few days later and stayed at a hotel within walking distance of the cathedral. As we ventured out that morning, I noticed a Security Service man watching us, which wouldn't be the last time we'd be followed by Security Service personnel. The cathedral was a major tourist attraction and the line to get in was quite long. But, it was worth it. St. Vitus was an extraordinary place. In its day, it had been one of the largest Christian churches ever built, and it was in a beautiful state of preservation. We asked if we might be allowed to step out of the tourist line and sit in one of the pews to pray. Permission granted, so we positioned ourselves near the main altar. I think we were all expecting some kind of attack—after all, this was the heart of the occult phenomena. I sat at the ready, in full alert mode. The nine warrior spirits Pakal had loaned me were also available and ready for anything that might occur. My witnesses, on the other hand, were quite anxious, frightened by the possibility that they could be harmed by something they barely understood.

WHAT WANTS TO BE KNOWN

We sat there for a long while until it became clear that there would be no attack, that there was nothing defending the fulcrum of the dark occult triangle. It was defenseless. Dissolving it would be easy. I looked up and realized that the center point of the cathedral's ceiling was actually the entrance into this negative force field. I offered a loving and kind energetic, and after a period of time, the force field completely vanished.

The cathedral felt very different. It felt as though the center point of the ceiling opened up and a beautiful shower fell on me. A shower of summer rain, rain that held within it gifts of love, gifts of healing, gifts of capacity. As I received these gifts, I distributed them among my thirteen witnesses. And, then, I was given a gift of capacity that at the time I didn't understand. What I did understand, however, was this: From where I was sitting at St. Vitus, I could "visit" the church in Turin, the last side of the occult triangle and dissolve it, too, by offering gifts of love and kindness. Which I did.

We kept sitting in those pews, no one much interested in getting up. We had just experienced an overwhelming moment of kindness and abundance. Slowly we left the pews and proceeded to walk out of the church, following the tourists in front of us, who were blissfully unaware that anything out of the ordinary had occurred. As we left, the Dark Occult Triangle had been removed from Europe. Back out in the afternoon sun, each one of us was happy.

What I came to understand was that the Dark Occult Triangle had been co-opted by the Nazis and by the Stalinists, and each had used its force in their attempts to dominate and manipulate the higher vibrational realms of the Sacred.

So with this occult force field dissolved, the higher realms of the Sacred no longer had an interference which had been disturbing them.

CLEARING THE KILLING FIELDS

The morning after I had been at St. Vitus, I sat outside in the early morning sun, listening for what wanted to be known. I sat and waited, sat and waited some more. Finally, what wanted to be known revealed itself—and it was quite astonishing. The sense was that I had to visit a Nazi death camp. There happened to be one about thirty miles north of the city; a combination concentration camp and Jewish ghetto known as Terezin, contained within the walls of Theresienstadt, a fortress built in the late 18th century by Emperor Joseph II of Austria.

My witnesses and I arrived sometime in the late morning, or early afternoon. The parking lot was surprisingly crowded, full of the curious and the idlers, and at least a couple dozen motorcyclists, whose energy felt negative and hostile. I discovered that these bikers were feasting on the negativity at Terezin, energizing themselves on the horrors of World War II.

We made our way from the parking lot to what appeared to be the main area, and found ourselves in the middle of a huge cemetery. Each grave in the first hundred or so rows was decorated with fresh flowers; and the graves in the other rows were bare. The graves with the flowers were Czech national heroes; the graves without the flowers were dead Jews. Thousands died there; many thousands of others were held there until they could be transported to death camps such as Auschwitz where they were exterminated.

I offered blessings at the cemetery and I became quite overwhelmed. There were so many men, women, and children who had suffered so much and who had died horrible deaths. I wasn't sure I could proceed without completely collapsing from the pain. I was so emotional, so upset by what I was witnessing. And then, I began to feel the presence of both Gussie and don Manuel, who had shown up to offer their support, encouragement, and strength so I could get through. They often did that during my years in Europe, when the work became too much for me to handle physically or emotionally.

I did the best I could. When I was done offering blessings, I led my group of witnesses into the area where the prisoners had been held. Over the next several hours I went to every open door of every prison cell, I walked to every holding area and every torture site, and did my best to offer kindness and love, healing and cleansing, whatever I could manage to offer. I paused a number of times, there were so many souls, so many so-called 'ghosts,' still wandering around, confused, dazed, unclear what to do. It was thick with souls, and I was moved to ask them if they were ready to return home.

I realized that my obligation there was not only to offer clearings and healings but to assist the souls of the dead on their journey home. I watched as these souls rose and entered the light.

During the time we were there, the Camp felt lighter, more open, freer, less troubled. But, somehow, the less troubled the Camp became, the more troubled I became. By the time we left there in the late afternoon, I was exhausted and I knew it was time for me to leave Prague.

Prague's Security had been in the parking lot in Terezin, and I had sensed they were watching us from a discrete distance the entire time we were at the Camp. I began to wonder whether we'd be able to fly out the next morning. It brought me back to the first odd encounter I had in Europe—I think it was during my second visit there in the winter of 2000. I was in Normandy visiting some of the archaeological ruins, which were medieval in their origins. At one castle, I was standing against the wall, posing for a picture at the request of my hosts. After posing, I noticed a rather nondescript middle-aged man, watching me. He approached me, addressed me by name, and introduced himself. I had no idea how he knew me; after all, I was quite new to France, and I had been intent on keeping a low profile. He told me that he was an official of the Masons, and would like to invite me to dinner. The dinner wasn't particularly memorable. The man politely asked me what I was doing in Europe, what my plans were, what agendas I had. I was honest with him. I told him I had come to Europe as a result of a series of dreams. That I had no clear sense, at that point, what I was doing in Europe. I was simply waiting for information, waiting for what wanted to be be known. I'm sure this man thought I was being evasive. And I had no idea what he wanted from me. By the time dinner was over, I was pretty sure he was warning me that the Masons were still a force, and for whatever reason I was being watched.

So encountering Prague's Security didn't surprise me. They certainly weren't in the parking lot that day trying to prevent me from entering the Camp. Their presence was much more about the Dark Occult Triangle. How do I know this? Because, when I first found out about the Occult Triangle, I had been less than convinced about its presence. And then I met a second woman, who was also close to the Vatican. Sitting next to one another at dinner one evening, she confirmed the information I had received earlier from my Italian acquaintance, and reiterated quite pointedly that it was highly confidential, nowhere to be found historically. It was hidden information.

Even though I had known I was treading on thin ice, moving into forbidden terrain, I had gone to Prague anyway. I had stepped into the occult, which, like all things esoteric during the Soviet era, was considered the property of the State. Apparently, Prague Security still believed that it all needed to be protected and controlled in the Czech Republic.

Anyway, the next morning at the airport, Security was very much in evidence. I checked my bag and walked with one of my witnesses towards the gate area; I could see Security standing at the checkpoint. When I boarded the plane, I sat down next to the woman I had been walking with. I noticed she was a bit shaken up and I asked her what happened. She told me that, when we were walking toward that airport checkpoint, I suddenly disappeared. I was nowhere to be found. It seemed odd, she said, but she figured she'd just keep walking, go through security, and meet up with me when we boarded. Sure enough, there I was on the other side of the checkpoint, ready to board. She asked me why I disappeared, how that happened, and how I could have reappeared. I understood that her questions were merely rhetorical. I smiled, and the plane began its ascent.

Terezin was the first recipient of the gift of kindness I had received at St. Vitus and was obligated to pass on. That gift only intensified as

PART THREE: FULFILLING MY OBLIGATIONS

I continued offering prayers of kindness during the thirteen years of my pilgrimage—at Europe's military and civilian cemeteries, killing fields, concentration camps, battlefields, prisons, ghettoes, and public memorials.

One cold, rainy afternoon, we arrived at the Sava River in Croatia, to visit Jasenovac, a WWII concentration camp established by the Independent State of Croatia, and sometimes referred to as the Auschwitz of the Balkans. We checked in at the memorial office and after a lengthy conversation with the site supervisor, we paused to read from the lists of names of the dead in the official ledgers. The weather was dreary—heavy mist and fog—as we walked onto the memorial grounds and headed toward the Sava River. Just before we reached the river, I suddenly stopped. Overwhelmed by the horror, I fell to my knees, broke down and wept. Once again I felt the presence of Gussie and don Manuel and I was able to carry on. For me, Jasenovac was the most negative of all the locations I prayed at in Europe. Descriptions of its extraordinary barbarity haunt me to this day.

I continued my pilgrimage stopping at tombs, religious relics and killing fields. Often I was gifted with blessings and teachings. Back in Krakow we visited Saint Mary's Basilica. We headed down to a large room, underneath the main level of the Basilica, which is reserved for the honored dead. I stood off to one side of the room and, as I did so, I was bathed in a subtle energy that flowed out of the depths of the earth and gifted us with an extraordinary quality. The dampness of the room, the negativity emanating from the tombs, and the tourist crowding all faded as I danced in this delightful earth energy.

Over the years I have offered healings to land damaged by violence, chemical pollution, fire and overuse. I offered these healings in North America, Central America, South America, and Europe. And I have restored and cultivated the subtle energies of forests, beaches, and farmlands. Neither Gussie nor don Manuel offered land healings; this was a capacity I was born with. I have been doing this work since I was a teenager. I had initially set out, when I was about seventeen or eighteen, to clear the battlefields of Gettysburg, but it didn't go so well. I was too overwhelmed. The older I got, of course, and the more I committed to clearing the suffering, the better I got at it. I was able to cleanse the American Civil War battlefields in Northern Virginia and in Gettysburg in Pennsylvania, and release the souls that continued to wander around long after the battles were over. Those visits were an effort to lighten up the negativity around Washington D.C.

I also visited New Orleans and the Gulf region, post-Katrina, again trying to help them to heal. In Europe I visited killing fields, battlefields and innumerable cemeteries, where they buried their War dead. I visited the war dead in the States and at Arlington National Cemetery. I visited more than I can remember, releasing souls, clearing land, offering healings, doing what I could. I traveled tens of thousands of miles over the next ten years. Finally, in 2014, it became clear to me that I had done enough.

Liberating the Light Columns

My land healings and my efforts to free large numbers of souls who are wandering the planet actually began at a place called Chaco Canyon National Historic Park. Chaco Canyon, located in a remote area in northwestern New Mexico, is home to a vast collection of pre-Colombian ruins and is now on the endangered list. Unfortunately, the canyon is in a natural gas region, where drilling and pumping of natural gas is common. So, although the United Nations deemed it a World Heritage Site, Chaco continues to be threatened by the oil and gas industry.

At any rate, I started visiting Chaco well before the natural gas boom, sometime in the late 1980s or early 1990s. It has extreme weather, no tourist services, and the main access road is, for most of its distance, unpaved. I've camped there in all kinds of conditions: during a windstorm and a sandstorm; in the snow and in the blistering heat. I've probably been to Chaco at least twenty times over the years, lured there by its extraordinary beauty and by a mysterious energetic quality I found both stimulating and relaxing.

Chaco was the largest ceremonial pilgrimage site west of the Mississippi for at least a thousand years; archeologists now speculate that it may have also supported more permanent residents than they initially thought. What particularly interested me there was Fajada Butte, a landform that appeared to be an energetic generator, the source of the high vibrational quality of the canyon. Fajada was off limits to visitors; signs posted by the National Park Service kept us away, so we never got any closer than a mile or two. Whenever I'd go to Chaco, I'd spend at least a week or so and focus my attention on Fajada Butte, trying to open myself to fully experience it, and trying to fathom what it actually was.

I did this for several years and then, in the 2000s, I visited St. Mary's Basilica, a medieval church in Krakow. In the basement of that church I experienced a very strong Earth energy, an energy that seemed to well up from deep down in the bowels of the earth. On my next trip to Chaco, I remembered that Krakow church and I realized that Fajada was, in fact, similar. Energy buried deep within the bowels of the earth was welling up within Fajada Butte, too. I wondered whether that energy could be directly contacted.

WHAT WANTS TO BE KNOWN

So one afternoon, I sat as near as I could to Fajada and began offering it a direct relationship by mirroring the energy it was giving off. As it emanated toward me, I reflected it back on itself; it would come back at me and I would again reflect it back on itself. Each time I did that, I noticed that the energy was getting stronger. I was acting as a huge mirror that allowed Fajada to experience itself, and as it experienced itself it grew. It was as if it were waking up. It was as if it needed my consciousness in order to do that. It continued to grow until it became this massive high vibrational energy and began to spill out all over the canyon.

I had a sense that whatever Chaco was, whatever Fajada Butte was, it just needed structure, and once it had that it could somehow be renewed or reawakened. So I danced into it, delighted to play in its counterclockwise spiral, and it welcomed me. I became Fajada as Fajada became me. From inside this mass of intense energy, I pushed it upward, shaping it into a spinning column of intense bright energy that kept expanding, spiraling up from Earth's soul. I was restoring an energetic system of emanation and reflection, structuring it, awakening it in such a way that it could radiate all through the canyon and be reflected back on itself.

Fajada got taller until finally it grew so high that it reached the edges of Earth's energy field. I stayed with Fajada, keeping it structured as a light column, an up-welling of Earth vitality. The whole area of Chaco Canyon took on the quality that I suspect originally drew pilgrims to it a thousand years ago. After two or three days, this light column no longer needed me to hold it in place. Its structure had become solid and it was functioning quite well within the mirror system of the canyons. I could feel Chaco's healing energy, it's high vibrational, spiritual quality spreading out over the land. In fact, a few days later when I got back to the Albuquerque airport to return home, I could still feel Chaco. Its energetic quality was once again influencing a very large land area.

Shortly after I returned home from Chaco, I began to wonder about the Temple of Inscriptions at Palenque, the resting place of Lord Pakal. I knew the Temple of Inscriptions was a pyramid and underneath it was a huge Earth energy, much like that at Fajada Butte. I believed this Earth energy, this light column, could be summoned to once again flow up through the Temple and flood the ancient city of Palenque. So a few months later, I traveled to Palenque and invited the Temple of Inscriptions to wake up—I even videotaped that healing and later posted it on my website. After the light column was functioning, I connected it with the light column at Chaco and they formed a giant arch.

A couple of months later I went to the Temple of the Sun in Cusco, where once again, I invited energy lying dormant underneath the temple to wake up. When it was fully functioning, I connected it with the light columns at Chaco and the Temple of Inscriptions.

The next light column that needed my attention was in Krakow. So off I went, accompanied by one witness, Sasa Petejan, back again to the old church there, St. Mary's Basilica. When we got there, I stood across the street from the church, with my back against the wall, surveying the situation. Was there any danger in my entering? Did the church have any guardians, who might sense why I was there? I was not there to pray, I was not there as a tourist, I was not there out of curiosity. I had returned there, after having visited it before. Now I was there with a witness to liberate the light column, a huge energy field that the church was literally built on top of; an energy field it was diverting for its own purposes. I wanted that huge energy, which I referred to as the Light Column of Krakow, to be allowed to simply bubble up out of the ground, with no interference from the church, and do whatever it would naturally do.

I stood outside and I watched and I waited. I announced my presence; I announced what my intention was. I was not asking permission, however. I was simply saying that I would be entering the church momentarily to release its grip on that very powerful energy it had co-opted, almost a thousand years earlier. I continued to wait.

After about fifteen minutes, I slowly started to walk toward the entrance. But, before I went any farther, I asked Sasa to stand off to the side—just in case we were attacked. Truth was, I hadn't experienced any attack in Europe anywhere, during the thirteen or so years of this service to my teachers. But still, I asked her to move out of what could be the line of fire. Good thing I did, because just as I got within fifteen feet or so of the stone steps at the entrance, a very powerful bolt of lightning hurled from the top stair, heading right for me, intent on lodging itself in my midsection. The lightning bolt was traveling at great speed; as soon as it was launched I did a quick two-step to my right and it crashed into the wall behind me. A very powerful, if not deadly assault, to be sure, but oddly enough it was not capable of altering its course. So when I stepped away, it crashed into the building behind me.

I said hello to my challenger, a greeting that demanded it to remove itself or be destroyed. It was, as you might imagine, a spirit. A guardian spirit placed there long ago to guard the light column, co-opted by a certain lineage of priests, and to protect the church. That lineage had long since disappeared. An artifact of an earlier time in the history of St. Mary's, with no one to direct it, the spirit was now leaderless and purposeless. It simply disappeared after that and removed itself into the spirit world. All over Europe the priestly and the occult lineages that had created protection and defensive perimeters for what I was visiting, had long since died. None of them seem to have survived World War II, and I suspect they didn't survive World War 1 either. The Wars, the Nazis, the Soviets all took their toll on these lineages. So by the year 2000 when I started what I was doing, there were no lineages to confront me. It was all historic artifact.

Finally, at the Great Mosque at Cordoba I discovered the main light column, the principal column; the other eleven were subsidiaries. Once I restored it, the energy within the Great Mosque, became—and continues to be—the strongest energetic I've ever experienced. For those sensitive to this subtle energy fields, it can be overwhelming. From the energetics of the Great Mosque, I could see clearly where the remaining five light columns were. From its energy, from the Great Mosque's light column, I was able to wake up the remaining five light columns without having to be physically present at each location. All twelve light columns were now hooked up to each other.

These energetic arches, as up-welling columns of light, all meet at a midpoint above the planet's energy system and I have witnessed how all the spaces were filled in between. The arches generated and support a high vibrational field that encircles the planet. As this field started to form, I noticed that the columns of light all became connected to the earth's soul. So Earth soul, the columns of light that express Earth soul, and the field surrounding the planet that reflects Earth soul, form a system, a system that has been restored and is still intact today. This esoteric vibrational field has slowly freed millions of ghosts, millions of traumatized souls who have wandered the surface of the planet. They have been gently coaxed to go home.

I've also noticed a general lightning of negative places, a general clearing of Earth's trauma, a general healing in the natural world. This is the work of the kindness of Earth soul and its reflective field, a system that has not been in operation for at least a thousand years, and has now been restored. In the process we have largely become free of the clutter, difficulty, and confusion caused by the millions of souls wandering the earth, and by the Earth trauma that can often make it difficult to enjoy the natural world.

After all was said and done, I began to suspect that what I had been doing was living out the life path that had been set out for me by my lineages. I was, in some way, fulfilling the obligations of both don Manuel and Lord Pakal. As I mentioned earlier, don Manuel had gifted me with the knowledge of the most refined energies of the higher realms, which enabled me to access the subtle energy fields around the planet. Lord Pakal gave me the further capacity to command these subtle energies and also to create some myself. So I was able to transform the raw, crude energy of the twelve light columns into a highly refined, potent blending of subtle energies.

In retrospect, I realized that there had been a convergence between Lord Pakal and don Manuel. Both wanted a new time, in which there would be a repair, or healing, or rejuvenation of the higher reaches of the upper realms. Each gave me capacities that enabled me to fulfill my service. And in the end, there was a construction, or reconstruction, of the subtle energy field that now circles our planet and has brought a renewed vigor to the upper realms of the Sacred, and has helped to revive some of the more stagnant qualities of our Earth. All of that would not have been possible without the gifting of both of these Masters. I needed both. They both wanted me to do this, they had the same intention, and each gave me what their traditions allowed them to give.

PART FOUR

LISTENING TO WHAT WANTS TO BE KNOWN

Why, What, and How I Teach

After some time, I began to realize that there was no one in my family who was interested in our esoteric lineage and that the tradition would die with me. I didn't know what to do about it. I was just sad. The same thing happened when I stopped being a student of Don Manuel's and Lord Pakal's. I didn't want what I had learned from them to die with me. I knew I needed to take on students and offer my own interpretation of what I'd been taught, stripped of its cultural baggage so that it made sense in our modern world. I needed to give words to the wordless. Essentially, that was what I had promised don Manuel after he chose me to take his teachings to the West. The problem? I had no idea how to communicate with individuals in the secular world; I didn't understand it or ordinary American reality; and I certainly had trouble navigating the rhythms of the day.

I've known all this about myself since I was in my mid-twenties. All through grade school and high school I had friends I could hang out with; I spent lots of time going to movies, jazz clubs, and other events in the City, navigating the subways and buses to make that happen. But as I got older, I found it more difficult to relate to the world ordinary people lived in.

And yet, I wanted to teach, as one way of serving humanity. Esoteric teaching needs individuals, it needs social context. I do enjoy teaching—it's both gratifying and stimulating—and it also frustrates me. Often the people to whom I'm explaining esoteric spirituality have limited experience with this concept and often equate it with religion—when in fact it's not that. What they've experienced, what they know about, is a set of rules, processes and procedures designed in accordance with a particular belief system. Esoteric spirituality, the realm where I live, the practices I teach, have nothing to do with rules, procedures, or belief systems. It's about individuals living and acting in a direct way, amid the wonder, the grandeur, and mystery of "All That Is." It's about finding the courage to step out of all that shelters us and meet the Sacred.

I want to prepare and encourage individuals to experience the Sacred directly for themselves. I want them to understand that the way to do that is through service; service is the doorway that leads to a direct experience of the Sacred.

PART FOUR: LISTENING TO WHAT WANTS TO BE KNOWN

My teachers assumed that I would pass along what I was taught to a single person, someone I designated as an heir to their lineages. And then, that one student would pass the teachings along to one other person. But I don't have that one student. I have no heir. I finally decided to talk about what I've been taught—and to put it down in writing—in order to preserve as much as I could. Each time I take up a topic with my students, I go through the same internal monologue: Should I be talking about this? How much can I talk about? Is it really OK for me to be open? Since none of what I learned was communicated to me verbally, I had to figure out how to express what was never put into words for me; how to explain what I've never thought about or read about; how to make sense of what was communicated to me in dreams or visions. In order to do all that, I must always wait for what wants to be known.

All three of my teachers taught me telepathically; they taught by transmission. A transmission is a subliminal gifting of something that can be communicated better without words. A certain kind of smile delivers a message from one person to another without anyone saying a word; a look passes between two people and says all that needs to be said. Those are transmissions. Mine are simply more elaborate. Transmitting spiritual information telepathically is the traditional way because spiritual information is often hard to verbalize; words get in the way.

WHAT WANTS TO BE KNOWN

So, yes, there was never any need for my teachers to speak to me. I never asked any questions— questions were inappropriate and conversation impossible. There was never a "hello how are you?" Nothing like that ever occured. I had no idea how they were doing, or what was up with them, how their night had been, or how their health was. I had no idea what was going on with them, other than what was taking place in that moment. That's a traditional way.

I taught that way for years. I never spoke to my students about anything, never entertained questions. My teaching was 100 percent in silence. And then, one afternoon a few years ago, I was teaching in the high desert of Chaco. I became so frustrated with the pediatrician I was teaching that I just started talking to her directly. Her face lit up. She got it. And then I got it. The only way I could successfully teach Westerners was to offer a combination of verbal and non-verbal instruction. So now I offer transmissions and blessings and verbal instruction in my teaching— totally untraditional, but completely necessary in the West. I'm still learning how to teach Westerners, of course; I listen to what wants to be known, so that I can communicate more effectively and continue to be of service.

To be clear, I'm not teaching anyone how to be a healer—of the land or of souls, of physical ailments or emotional pain and suffering. I'm not teaching anyone how to be a shaman or how to inhabit the spirit world or the higher realms. I'm teaching individuals, in a post-modern world, how to come to the mystical way. And what that means is this. If you want to experience All That Is, if you want to have a relationship with the Sacred, you have to stop being so self-absorbed—so inward—get outside of yourself, and be of service. I know that may sound a little harsh, but it's true. Getting stuck in your own head, in your own problems constitutes the biggest roadblock to seeing what's outside of yourself; if you can't do that, it becomes almost impossible to see and respond to the suffering in the world.

When we let ourselves respond to suffering, when we are able to offer service, we can begin to experience an entire, extraordinary universe of possibilities beyond the confines of our own mind. It's not always easy to remove the obstacles that keep us separate from what is outside of ourselves. We may have too many projections, too many opinions we can't let go of; we may be too caught up in the chatter of our own minds. But fundamentally, as I tell my students, I believe that we have the capacity to respond to suffering. We have a built-in capacity for kindness and compassion, which allows us to notice the natural world and relate in more meaningful ways to other humans, and to nature. I believe—and the wisdom teachings I teach support that belief—that we have a capacity not only for kindness and compassion, but for reverence, respect for other people and for the natural world. When we honor that capacity, we become capable of experiencing the Sacred, without getting caught up in any belief systems or any particular cultural baggage.

In the following pages, I attempt to put into words the teachings I have received, to explore what it means to listen to what wants to be known, and to encourage others to enter into the realm of the Sacred, which means to always be of service.

Knowing
the Sacred

Entering into a relationship with the Sacred requires us to reestablish a skill set that is part of our human inheritance. We must move toward it with stillness and a sense of reverence and without projections. Listen and it will reveal itself in this stillness and reverence. What does this all mean? Where can we find the Sacred?

Central to my teaching and in the indigenous teachings of North and South America is the sense that we meet the Sacred outside of ourselves—not within. What I mean by "outside" is the vast, natural world in which we live, a world that is alive and active, a repository of energy, vibrations, and emanations, which exists independent of us. And the only way to meet the Sacred is to be in relationship with it, with the vastness and the particularities of everything that exists outside of us—the bird songs, the grasses, the trees, the mountains, the lakes, the skies, the planets, the stars in the whirling galaxies.

Surprisingly, the Sacred is quite relational. It won't be relational on our terms, it's relational only on its terms, which we have to discover. And we discover them by making whatever efforts we can to meet the Sacred. But, let's get this out of the way now: In spite of your best efforts, the Sacred will never become your friend or your ally. It will not protect you. It will not help you grow emotionally. In fact, the Sacred will do nothing for you. There is no personal advantage in meeting the Sacred and establishing a relationship with it. I know that's difficult for a lot of humans because we are self-serving, self-seeking, on the look out for what's best for ourselves, what will serve our further growth and development. Our relationship with the Sacred is a choice we make that cannot be motivated by self-interest.

So what would motivate you to want a relationship with the Sacred? For many it's the realization that every attempt to find the Sacred within has brought endless frustration and culminated in self-absorption and suffering. The antidote to all that, of course, is to extend ourselves relationally, reverently to a visible manifestation of the Sacred, the natural world, a world that is actually open to us; that is oddly inviting, beckoning, welcoming, and alternately benign and dangerous. A natural world that, if you attempt to meet it, may even respond to you in surprising ways. The natural world, of course, has an aesthetic that has traditionally attracted Westerners — the land, the sheer beauty of the rivers and lakes, mountains and valleys; the sense of aliveness in the jungles, woods and oceans; the great trees and the great deserts. It's endless. The New World in all its vastness continues to attract us. But in order to really be in relationship to All That Is, we must stop being tourists, onlookers in the natural world and enter into it fully.

We can't possibly know what nature needs until we understand what nature is. It's true that no sustainable relationship can exist without reciprocity; no meaningful relationship can exist without reverence, but herein lies the difference: In the Western "let us fix it" model, we are projecting onto nature what we believe she is (and, by extension what we believe she needs) without ever allowing her to show us. The traditional understanding, which is the way I teach, is that reality is mystical; it is the essence of direct experience. It is not an inventory of characteristics. The key is to allow what wants to be known to come to you over time.

The fact is, we're not paying enough attention to nature to even know what she needs—or, most important, who she is. Even when we're outside, in nature, we separate ourselves by plugging into music or podcasts, hiding behind the camera, or myriad other distractions. All of this also keeps us from seeing the effects of our inattention and carelessness. How are we to notice the consequences of our actions if we're not truly engaged with the natural world, if we fail to understand that we are part of nature, not apart from it? Who is to care for the planet going forward? How do we engage with the natural world when we have almost no awareness of her, beyond perhaps an aesthetic appreciation?

It's helpful to remember that our ancestors once lived as part of the natural world and understood themselves to be an intimate part of it. Humans today have almost no direct experience of the natural world and therefore almost no direct experience of the Sacred. But our species is capable of this connection because it is our natural inheritance as humans. Entering into this relationship with the Sacred requires us to reestablish a skill set that is part of this inheritance. To do this, we must approach the Sacred more as a poet, and less as a scientist. Remember, the natural world is radically neutral. We must move toward it with stillness and a sense of reverence and without projections. Listen and it will reveal itself in this stillness and reverence. Not necessarily in an hour or two or even in a year or two. You must listen and look without expectation. The natural world is not human and will be experienced only as you become more open and empty as a receiver. And yet, it is a deeply human experience, one that connects us to the world we are born into and the sacredness of everything around us.

PART FOUR: LISTENING TO WHAT WANTS TO BE KNOWN

We meet the spirits of the natural world, we delight in the gifts we receive, and then we're obligated to give back. Ours is a reciprocal relationship. It's not about us taking what we can get to feel better. We have to be willing to give gifts. And you will discover what gifts you have to give. You will also discover all of the challenges of being in relationship to something that is not human and rarely responds the way humans respond. All of the dilemmas we've had in relating to each other rise to the surface when we enter into relationships with the natural world. We may even discover that we haven't been very good at relationships and we have a lot to learn.

The Practice of Deep Listening

The traditional way of accessing the Sacred is not out of the realm of possibility for any of us. It requires us to listen for what wants to be known. This is a type of listening without our projections, our internal conversation, our impressions, our thoughts, our feelings. It requires us to listen patiently and quietly in the late night silence, inside the early morning breezes, and in the murmurings of creeks; to be open to receiving whatever arises. This is a skill set that needs to be cultivated over many months and years. At first, you may hear nothing but your own breath. Then you may believe you hear something but you don't trust it because you don't know what it should sound like.

Try listening to birds, to the wind, to the waves at the beach, to the silence of the night sky, the grasses as you walk, or the hum of rush hour traffic. The point is: Listen to what is outside of your-

PART FOUR: LISTENING TO WHAT WANTS TO BE KNOWN

self and wait patiently for whatever is presented. Be patient enough to allow yourself to reclaim a skill set you had as a young child when you sat and watched the ripples in a pool of water, or listened to the rain, giggled with your dog or cat, laughed with the wind, or rolled in the grass. Try playing in the grass or at the beach with children, allowing their simple, naïve openness to help you rediscover a sense of joy, wonder, and relatedness.

Listening to what wants to be known may open us to something elusive that now wants our attention, to the deeper wisdom available to all of us. Perhaps we may come to know what is hidden behind the veil, what our wise teachers have tried to invite us into, and what Earth itself is inviting us into. Come, listen deeply, and listen closely like you did as a child when you knew the Sacred and knew it was outside of yourself.

Listening to what wants to be known is to listen within the sounds of a baby's laughter, a creek, a sonata, or a train whistle. Inside, go inside the sounds. And how do I go inside, you ask? What is the procedure, the technique? This question has no direct answer. Try to be quiet, calm yourself, relax your nervous system and stop asking questions. You already know how to listen.

Deeper listening is a skill set that is part of our species intelligence. We have had the capacity to listen to the natural world, a capacity that has served us for millennia when we lived intimately within nature. We knew what birds were saying and we understood the speech of the wind. Now we have to 'remember' or recover this skill set.

I recall an afternoon walk with a friend, a native man who knew the language of birds. As we walked, he noticed a hawk circling us making loud noises. My friend stopped, turned to me, and said that the hawk told him we were in danger at that very moment. As we looked around, we saw a very large cat who, as we watched it, was certainly stalking us.

Listening deeply opens us to information otherwise unavailable. What we learn depends on the quality of our listening, our experience as a listener, and our ability to accept what we've learned, no matter how uncomfortable we are with the information presented. With patient practice, our listening skills may begin to access terrain that is outside of time, within which is information of a deeper character. This terrain, with its timelessness and ongoing present tense, is where we come to experience the surprising revelations of sacred speech. Here, we may learn about the interiority of the natural world and the deeper wisdom of the all that is. What wants to be known will continue to insist on being known.

Sometimes our dreams give us an opportunity to listen to sacred speech. These dreams have an unusual character. They may feel like your dreams, because you are the dreamer, and yet they contain unfamiliar content. Dreams that contain sacred speech can be listened to in the same way that you would listen to the wind or the cries of a hawk. The organ of listening—our ears—opens to the gentle whispers of the deeper truth that wants to be known.

When you meet the Sacred, you must meet it with a profound sense of reverence, honoring its preciousness and its extraordinary and unique qualities. Approach it with great care, great respect, and great wonder, as though you were meeting a newborn baby for the first time.

Listening to what wants to be known is to listen to what demands to be heard. But we can't hear this demand if we remain aloof, distracted by busyness or plagued by doubts. Start with what's readily available. Find a tree that resonates with you and stand next to it, feeling your back against its trunk. Listen. Wait. Feel its aliveness. Feel its connection to the earth. Experience its 'pulse.' Now take a photo of that tree. Keep it with you, or put it up on your mirror or wall. There was a time when I had many photos of trees, mountains, rivers, and beaches in my house. I was in the process of developing relationships with them, and these visual "prompts," as I like to call them, really helped me maintain contact with them throughout the day.

As we deepen our listening, we may discover that what wants to be known is the preciousness of daily life, lived with respect, gratitude, and joy. Living life in the Sacred is to live each moment with reverence, a sense of appreciation for

All That Is. Our appreciation, our empathy, our caring, is our gift to the Sacred. Mysteriously, the Sacred does respond to us in a language which is intuitively familiar in its fluidity and playfulness.

As you continue to listen to what wants to be known, you may discover, as I did, that although the Sacred is not concerned with your wellbeing or personal growth, it may, on occasion and unpredictably, respond to personal prayer. So do not mistake its radical neutrality as indifference. Remember, its impact on daily life is complex, nuanced, unpredictable, and uncontrollable.

The Sacred is truly concerned but the terms of its concern are not human.

The Soul's Journey

If we ask "who" is listening, we can get caught up in conversations about the "self," "the higher self," or even a psychologized "listener." Perhaps a more useful question is "What is listening?". Is it the intellect, the personality, or the body/being? Is it something else within you that is capable of listening and experiencing and establishing a relationship with the Sacred?

Traditionally, in the West we have believed that each of us has a sacred essence or spark, a soul that is with us at birth and leaves us when the body dies. It is our soul that is capable of learning to listen to sacred speech without intellectualizing or psychologizing its meanings. And, as the soul learns to be a better listener, it becomes more aware. So spiritual development—the progress of the spiritual seeker—is a process of awareness of the soul as it remains present in each moment. Our body, our intellect, and our psychology are all capable of supporting soul development as we care for our physical health, discipline our intellect's hunger, and reign in our psychological projections.

We become more able listeners as we become more respectful, more reverent. Slowly, our reverence evolves into a capacity for empathetically communing with sacred speech. In response, all of nature—birds, creeks, oceans, plants—reveals itself to be relationally capable of responding to our soul. Our soul's awareness, its consciousness, now experiences the natural world as conscious.

As our soul becomes more conscious, it becomes capable of directing our daily life. The soul's capacity, its 'operating system' is wordless, thoughtless and congruent with the imperatives of the higher levels of the Sacred. It's able to guide the individual to be actively concerned and reverent. This capacity of the soul to govern action simplifies the individual's life amidst the conflicting demands of the Sacred and the secular.

The soul's operating system, its capacity to function, is informed by what wants to be known. As it matures, it will become anchored in the timeless moral and ethical clarity of the All That Is, from which it is sourced. This information flow, which we often call 'wisdom,' is gentle, neutral, accepting and concerned.

The soul's operating system, with its absence of self-interest, expresses the wisdom of the All That

Is in the simplicity and reverence of our daily life. Daily life can be lived within the ordinary secular world or in the withdrawn venues of temples, ashrams and monasteries. Whatever the venue, the soul's actions will increasingly demonstrate an ascetic subtext.

Perhaps the soul's 'listening' becomes more refined because the soul's purpose has emerged. Then its operating system may begin to ask for guidance from All That Is. As this process of 'listening' and 'guidance' unfolds, the soul may become an agent of All That Is.

Since the soul's operating system is not self-aware, we can only surmise its purpose from the outside, observing how each individual soul chooses to express the wisdom of All That Is in daily life. Perhaps as the soul becomes more refined we can observe it expressing itself as the poet/scholar, healing icon, social activist, or contemplative. Each of these 'social types' is, of course, quite mutable as the soul continues to mature, especially if the soul's boundaries weaken or dissolve and it is absorbed within All That Is.

Our Species Wisdom

As we become more fluent, listening to what wants to be known can become an unfolding of extraordinary abundance. The listener may be treated to sudden bursts of surprising information, revelations, which seem to arrive fully articulated. What wants to be known, what must be known now during this time of chronic crisis, is the wisdom of our species.

Our species wisdom has never been static. Rather, it continues to accumulate as our social and cultural experience interacts with our species 'hard wiring.' Our species survival within a changing natural world, during the last 50,000 years, attests to the growth of our species wisdom. However, our current planetary confusion, ambivalence, and inaction can be attributed to our modern and postmodern ignorance of species wisdom.

PART FOUR: LISTENING TO WHAT WANTS TO BE KNOWN

Our contemporary ignorance of species wisdom has become a subject in popular culture. Do you know what to do in an avalanche or flood? In his book, Deep Survival, Laurence Gonzales' lecture is aimed at reconnecting us with our natural instincts. Perhaps you are trying to discover a more 'natural' diet like the Paleo diets. Or, have you forgotten how to track animals? Tom Brown's tracker books reacquaint us with our hunter skills.

Surprisingly, our species wisdom has also resurfaced in our growing respect for nature that has inspired recent legal and legislative initiatives. The granting of limited legal rights to primates in some jurisdictions of the United States and the granting of personhood, with full legal rights, to a national park in New Zealand are encouraging examples of our renewed reverence for the natural world.

Listening to species wisdom we discover two broad categories of information and teaching: how do I survive in this moment and how do I thrive in this moment. What we hear is surprising, revelatory, often counterintuitive, and culturally, context specific.

Access to species wisdom begins when we re-establish an intimate relationship with the materiality of the earth and an intimate relationship with our own physicality.

Wisdom That Has No Name

Underneath or surrounding our species wisdom is the wisdom that has no name, the wisdom of the All That Is. This is a wisdom that presents itself as divine revelation to skilled listeners, those who have the "eyes to see and the ears to hear."

Careful listening allows us to distinguish the wisdom that has no name from species wisdom. Species wisdom informs the actions of the soul's operating system; the wisdom without a name offers the soul its purpose and meaning and also demands its service. Unlike the dynamic quality of species wisdom, the wisdom of all that is continues to be known, unchanged, in all its simplicity and complexity.

This nameless wisdom has made itself known to me in dreams, on pilgrimage, at tombs, at churches and temples, in books, and during a lifetime of contact with teachers. What has wanted to be known is what my soul has needed to know in order to serve the All That Is. My continuing access to this wisdom is in the context of my ongoing service rather than my personal development.

Not everyone has access to the reservoir of nameless wisdom. As best I can tell, when access is granted, it is almost always limited or partial, even to the most elevated members of our species. For me, access was granted to specific domains of this wisdom by embodied and disembodied teachers and saints who gave me permissions on condition that I not misuse this wisdom. And along with these permissions has been a demand that I offer active service to the All That Is.

My continuing access to the wisdom with no name is within the context of my ongoing service to the All That Is. Personal and spiritual development may grant an abstract knowledge of the All That Is, but having abstract knowledge of All That Is is not the same as having direct access to it.

Afterword

I was taught within three esoteric traditions: the folk healing of the Yiddish shtetl, the shamanic healing of the Andes, and the planetary awareness of the Maya. I am careful not to appropriate the cultures of these traditions, so I simply self-identify as a spiritual healer and teacher, and practice, as best I can, the essence of these traditions. I am especially sensitive to being called a shaman because I do not live in a cultural context that supports shamanic practice.

With my healings, my teachings, my public talks, and my writing I have attempted to convey the mystery that is at the heart of these traditional practices and to hint at the deeper meaning of injunctions such as 'get in your body,' 'get grounded,' 'get a sense of place.' We have no cultural context for these injunctions so they became, over

AFTERWORD

the years, a California cliché.

I admit to my love of adventure. So, yes, this book is a 'romance,' an adventure, off the map and into a dangerous and uncharted region of the Andes before GPS tracking. Since then, the war ended in Peru and the Peruvian government has built a road to Q'eros for tourists. There is still adventure in the Andes but the traditional culture is in radical decline.

I continue to live in the counties immediately north of San Francisco. Occasionally, I meet Peruvians up here from the small towns and rural areas of the Andes. They are often suspicious and afraid of me. And local indigenous people wonder if I am a 'poisoner.' We holders of traditional power are not well received because so many of us have used our capacity to manipulate and harm.

Have I revealed any of the secret practices of the traditions I was trained in? Of course not because my training was all unspoken. Techniques, processes, and systems were all offered telepathically and, most importantly, teaching was simply an invitation to imitate the teacher. I have posted a few talks and healings on the internet. I also have a large archive which is password protected.

I'm a reader who enjoys books. I hope you enjoyed this read. It is all the truth.

Acknowledgments

Some years ago, Carmen Arróspide asked me to document my relationship with don Manuel Quispe, which lead to my first book, *Activist Mysticism*. After it was published, I had to admit that it didn't really work as a document of my time with my teacher.

Fast forward to 2016 at an annual weeklong retreat in northern California. One evening, with dinner over and evening chatter beginning, one of my students asked me a question about my life. One question begat another and another. Finally, as we wound down, Sue Priolo commented that my stories about my teachers would make an interesting book. A year later, at the next retreat Sue and her husband Carl reiterated that my stories would make a great book and they both volunteered to help. So once a week, they would come

ACKNOWLEDGMENTS

to my office with a list of questions and record my answers. Recordings were transcribed and then Carl fact-checked them against the original audio recordings for accuracy. Gene Novagratsky helped out with the tedium of fact-checking more that a year's worth of these recordings.

These transcripts were then passed on to Linda Sparrowe who has crafted a coherent book out of my stories. Linda was kind enough to write the foreword, and then off the book went to Girija Brilliant for proofing and then on to Sarah Keough and Ralph McGinnis (of R&S Media) for design and layout. Sarah appeared one rainy afternoon to take my photo for this book so I had an opportunity to also thank her for creating my new website.

This book was inspired by Sue and Carl Priolo and they also managed its preparation together. This was the last project of Sue and Carl's forty-year collaboration. Sue died before the manuscript went to press and I have tearfully dedicated it to her. My wife, Patricia, somehow tolerated all the time and expense. My teenage son, Teo, is deep into his own interests but may someday read this book.

About Paul

Born into a family of Yiddish visionaries and healers, Paul became heir at birth to his Grandmother Gussie's Central European lineage. From the time he was three, Paul spent hours every day sitting by Gussie's side, watching as she conducted numerous healings in complete silence. He learned to mirror and embody her skills, to offer healings the way she did, and to protect himself from the dangers found on the streets in the Bronx of the 1940s.

Years later, realizing he needed further training, an old friend suggested they venture to Peru. It was there, at a remote spiritual festival in the Andes that he found what he didn't even know he was looking for—don Manuel Quispe, an Andean high priest of the Q'eros people. Upon being introduced, don Manuel asked Paul a mysterious question: "What took you so long?" Although Paul had never heard of don Manuel, he agreed to spend time with him in his village. Over the next several years, don Manuel gave him silent transmissions nightly and specific tasks to complete. He then deemed Paul his heir and sent him back to the West to complete his work.

For more than seventy years, Paul has followed the directives of his grandmother Gussie and offers healings to anyone in need. For more than twenty-five years, he has furthered the mission of don Manuel by performing land-healing rituals all over the world. Central to Paul's work is his belief that to be developed spiritually, one needs to commit to a life of service.

Many see Paul as a powerful, modern-day shaman. He refers to himself, instead, as a companion to the land, which is the native way, and a traditional healer. He communicates directly with nature; he sees reality as reality. He listens to what needs to be known and proceeds accordingly. This was how don Manuel taught him; this is how he teaches; this is how he heals others. He is the culmination of all the silent gifting, teachings, and capacities he has received and he is, in turn, offering us teachings and transmissions online and in print.

Paul has lived and taught in the Bay Area since the mid-1980s. He continues to offer healings—in person, through photographs, and online. As famously reclusive as Paul is, people all over the world seek him out for his healings, his teachings, and his advice, including parents, students, celebrities, and high-powered Silicon Valley executives.

CPSIA information can be obtained
at www.ICGtesting.com
Printed in the USA
LVHW031047060120
642629LV00006B/617/P